13 GREAT DESIGNS FRO[M]

HOOKED [...]

Handbags & Totes

Contributors

Ali Strebel

Nola Heidbreder

Linda Pietz

Jennifer O'Malley

Norma Batastini

Sharon A. Smith

Cindy Irwin

Susan Clarke

Jen Manuell

Presented by

RUG HOOKING

Published by
AMPRY PUBLISHING LLC
3400 Dundee Road, Suite 220
Northbrook, IL 60062
www.amprycp.com

www.rughookingmagazine.com

Printed in the United States of America

10 9 8 7 6 5 4 3 2 1

Photography of completed pocketbooks by Kathleen Eckhaus

Process photographs by the artists

ISBN 978-1-945550-03-4

Library of Congress Control Number: 2017930015

CONTENTS

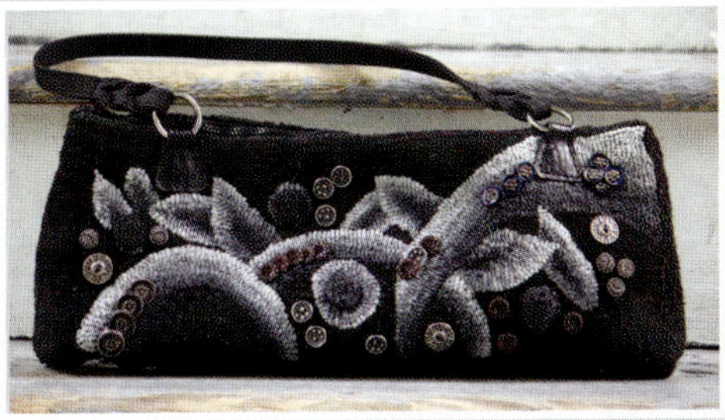

INTRODUCTION

HANDBAGS AND TOTES, CARPETBAGS AND PURSES.

These are staples in our daily lives. We carefully pick just the right one, the one that is a perfect reflection of our style, color sense, and personality. We might have a funky informal bag for a casual summer vacation and a structured, sophisticated purse for going to the office or attending important meetings.

These fashion accessories say a lot about us.

Why not say even more about yourself by sporting a hand-hooked bag? You know you want one. Remember the last time you saw one at a rug show or a hook-in? Do you recall that marvelous carpetbag you saw when you were traveling last summer? Were your fingers itching to make one for yourself?

This is your opportunity. *Hooked Carpetbags, Handbags & Totes* brings you the best designs from 9 of the premier designers in the rug hooking world today. This book is a compendium of 13 projects, from relaxed to structured, from funky to classic, all set forth to guide you as you finally make your very own hooked handbag. Or, if you are already a member of the society of hooked handbags with one or two tucked away in your closet, this is an opportunity to indulge yourself with another!

Rug Hooking magazine is pleased to present to you our latest collection of fabulous creations. Carry your hooked bag with pride!

Debra Smith
Editor

HOOKER'S DRAWSTRING BAG

Designed, hooked, and constructed by Ali Strebel

DIMENSIONS
6 1/2" x 8"

EVERYONE NEEDS A SMALL BAG TO HOLD SPECIAL TREASURES. This easy bag is great for all kinds of uses; I use it to hold my favorite hooks.

This bag saves you time and wool because you are only going to hook the motif, and you hook through wool rather than through linen. Hooking into wool is not any more difficult than hooking into any other rug backing. It is fun to simply hook the motif without having to plan a background. This charming bag is simple and quick to make—perfect to whip up as a gift. Or keep it for yourself to hold those hooks!

Preparation:

Using a chalk pencil, draw a 7 ½" x 9" rectangle in the center of the wool you will be hooking into. Next, draw the floral motif in the center of the rectangle, approximately 2 ½" from the top. (This 2 ½" provides space for the drawstring casing.)

Hooking:

Gently stretch the wool on your frame and hook the floral motif. I also hooked my initials on the back of the bag. Steam your completed hooking.

MATERIALS

Wool

- When finished, the hooked wool will measure 7 ½" x 9", but one piece needs to be larger in the beginning—it needs to be large enough to fit on your frame to make it easy for you to complete the hooking
- Wool strips: use leftovers from other projects. You won't need many, just enough to hook the simple flower motif

Lining: 2 pieces of 7 ½" x 9"cotton fabric

Drawstring: 2 pieces of yarn, each 25" long

Chalk pencil

Construction:

1. Once the hooking is complete, cut out the 7 ½" x 9" rectangle. Place the right sides together, and with ½" seams, sew the hooked piece to the wool backing, leaving the top open. Then sew the 2 cotton lining pieces together the same way, leaving a 2" opening along one side.
2. Place the lining pocket inside the wool pocket, with right sides together. Sew around the top edge, ¼" from the top. Turn the bag right side out: pull the hooked part and the lining through the opening you left in the lining side seam. Hand sew the opening closed.
3. Press the bag flat, paying special attention to the top seam.
4. To form the drawstring casing, sew around the top of the bag, ½" down from the top edge. Sew around again, down another ½" from the previous stitching.
5. Carefully snip an opening, through the wool only, on both of the side seams. Thread one piece of the yarn through the opening, in on one side and out again on the same side. Then, with the other piece of yarn, do the same thing from the other side. Knot the ends of the yarn. Strengthen the side seams that you snipped open with a few small stitches so that they do not unravel.
6. Place your special hooks inside, draw it up closed, and you are ready to go!

See pattern on page 94.

BOHEMIAN BANDED BAG

Designed, hooked, and constructed by Ali Strebel

DIMENSIONS
12" x 14 $\frac{1}{2}$"

EVERY ONCE IN A WHILE, THE OLD HIPPIE IN ME SHOWS UP, USUALLY IN MY ACCESSORIES. Those were the days—free and easy and unstructured. I love the way this bag turned out. It makes me smile when I carry it. And when my daughters thought it was cool I knew I had a winner! Have a little fun and make one for yourself.

MATERIALS

Linen backing: 12" x 24"

Wool

- 2 pieces for bag bottom: 12" x 14"
- Leftover wool strips from other projects for hit-or-miss hooking

Lining: 2 pieces of 12" x 14"cotton fabric

Yarn: coordinating colors for embellishments

Handles: 2 leather straps, each 30" long

4 D-rings

Preparation:

Using the 12" x 24" piece of rug linen, draw a 3 ½" x 20" rectangle on the linen backing, leaving 2 ½" at the bottom. (The extra linen at the top will be folded to the inside to make the lining when the hooking is completed.) Using the triangle pattern provided, fill in the rectangle with zigzag lines to guide your hooking.

Hooking:

Hook the zigzag pattern in a hit-or-miss fashion.

Construction:

With the hooking completed, press. Then trim away the bottom, leaving ¾". To form the band, fold this piece in half with right sides together. Sew the edges together using a zipper foot; sew as close to the hooking as possible. Set aside.

HOOKED BAND AND FRINGE, 3 ½" x 20"

BAG BOTTOM:

Preparation:
Use the diagram to construct a pattern for yourself. Trace around the pattern onto one piece of wool and one piece of cotton lining.

Construction:
1. Place the two wool pieces right sides together; sew on the chalk line. Do the same with the two lining pieces. Press.
2. Sew a gathering stitch around the top of each bag to make it easier to put the pieces together.
3. Put the lining bag inside the wool bag, wrong sides together.

Joining the hooked band to the bag bottom:
This can be a bit tricky. Take your time and it will work.
1. Pin the bag bottom to the hooked band, right sides together. Use the gathering thread on the bag bottom to fit the two together.
2. With a zipper foot, sew the two together as close to the hooking as possible.
3. Turn right side out, and fold the excess linen (the linen above the hooking) to the inside, covering the back of the hooking and the sewn seam.
4. Fold the raw edges under just a bit; hand stitch the band in place.

FINISHING:

1. Now embellish with the yarn. Whip stitch the top edge (like you would a rug).
2. Add fringe in two simple steps: hand stitch large loops under the hooking all the way around the bag, then cut all the loops. Instant fringe!

3. Sew the 4 D-rings by hand to the inside of the bag, approximately 2 ½" from the sides, both the front and back. Loop the leather straps through the D-rings and sew to secure. You can either sew these to the bag by machine or you can lace them together by hand. (A shoe repair store will sew them for a small fee.)

See pattern on page 95.

"FLOWER POWER" HANDBAG

Designed by Linda Pietz

Hooked and constructed by Nola Heidbreder

DIMENSIONS
14" x 9 ½"

EVERY SUMMER, OUR PATIO WAS AWASH WITH A MASS OF ORANGES, PINKS, AND REDS BECAUSE OUR MOTHER ALWAYS PLANTED ZINNIAS IN THE LATE SPRING. Unlike the lofty rose, there is something about this humble flower that puts a smile on your face. The zinnia brings back memories of sitting amidst those flowers on warm summer evenings as lightning bugs lazily swarmed around us, flashing merrily.

It was the 1960s, a time when Flower Power was all the rage. The counterculture of the time was full of flower power. Fashion embraced it, and there wasn't one article of clothing that didn't sport a field of brightly colored flowers—including purses. Always on the cutting edge of fashion, our mother even had a swimming cap covered with plastic flowers.

Our purse is a nostalgic nod to the fashions of the 1960s and a tribute to Mom and all those zinnias she planted and her fashion-forward style. We know she'd love this purse and we hope you will too.

MATERIALS

2 notches pink wool (a notch is 6" x 16")

4 notches red wool

3 notches orange wool

8 notches blue-green wool

Paint-on rug backing: we used Safety Back by MCG Textiles

Needle

Silver marker

Sewing thread to match cotton fabrics and lining of the purse

1/4 yd. fabric for lining (blue-green)

3 1/4 yd. of golden brown cotton fabric

Plastic purse form (available from Let Nola Do It)

Handles of your choice

Yarn for drawstring

One of each of the following Clover Yo-Yo Makers:

- 8708 Jumbo
- 8703 Extra Large
- 8701 Large
- 8700 Small

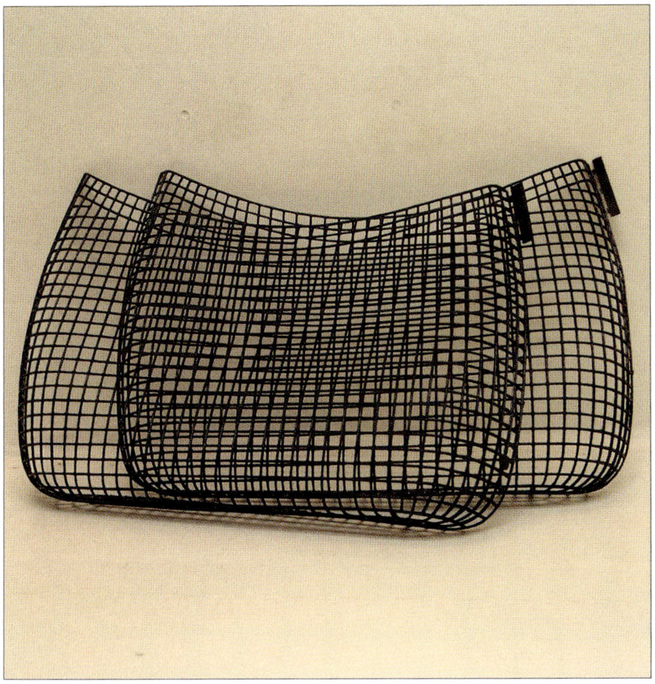

Preparation

1. Lay the plastic purse form on top of the pattern and trace the circles using a silver marker.
2. Make flower centers with the golden brown cotton fabric, using different size yo-yo makers. Choose one pattern of cotton for each of the petal colors. Match up the flower centers with the circles marked on the purse form.
3. Sew flower centers in place, sewing around the edges. Use a doubled piece of thread that matches the flower centers.
4. Cut each notch of the red, orange, and pink into 8 strips lengthwise. Cut each of these strips into 6 pieces, each about 2 ½" to 2 ¾" long. Shape the ends to resemble petals.
5. Prod the petals of the flowers around the flower centers using your fingers. With a petal in one hand on the outside of the purse and one hand on the inside of the purse, insert a petal into a hole in the plastic form close to the yo-yo center. Pull the petal halfway through to the inside of the purse. Insert the petal end into an adjacent hole, pulling the other half of the petal to the outside. Repeat this around the outside of the yo-yo to complete a flower. Be sure that each petal shares a hole with the petal next to it.
6. Sew sides of the form together, overlapping sides about 1 inch. Use heavy thread in either black or dark green.

Hooking:

1. Use a size #11 Bee Line Cutter blade to cut background wool, or cut the wool in ¾" wide strips. Hook remaining background using cool greens to blue greens. You will have to hook through two layers where the purse halves overlap.
2. Paint the interior of the purse with paint-on rug backing. This paint will seal the inside of the linen to prevent the hooking and proddy from coming out.

Construction:

1. Lining: Use the same blue-green fabric to line purse as was used for the background of the zinnias. Cut out two halves using the pattern. Sew in darts.
2. With right sides together, sew around the outer edge of the lining pieces, with a ½" seam allowance, leaving the top edge open. Turn ½" of the top edge over to the wrong side and press.
3. Place lining into purse with wrong side of lining against the wrong side of the hooked purse.
4. Sew the top edge of the lining to the loops of hooking at the top to hide the plastic edging. Make sure to use doubled thread.
5. Attach your chosen handles. Hand sew them to the outside of the bag with the waxed linen thread that comes with the handles.

See patterns on pages 96–97.

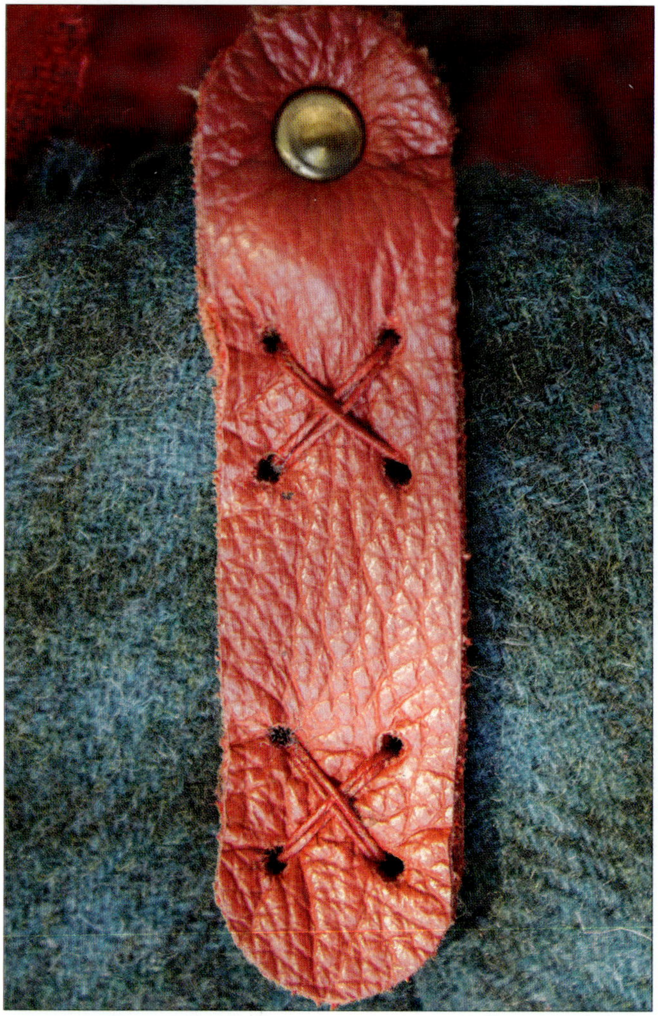

FOLK ART FLOWER TRAVEL TOTE

Designed by Linda Pietz

Hooked and constructed by Nola Heidbreder

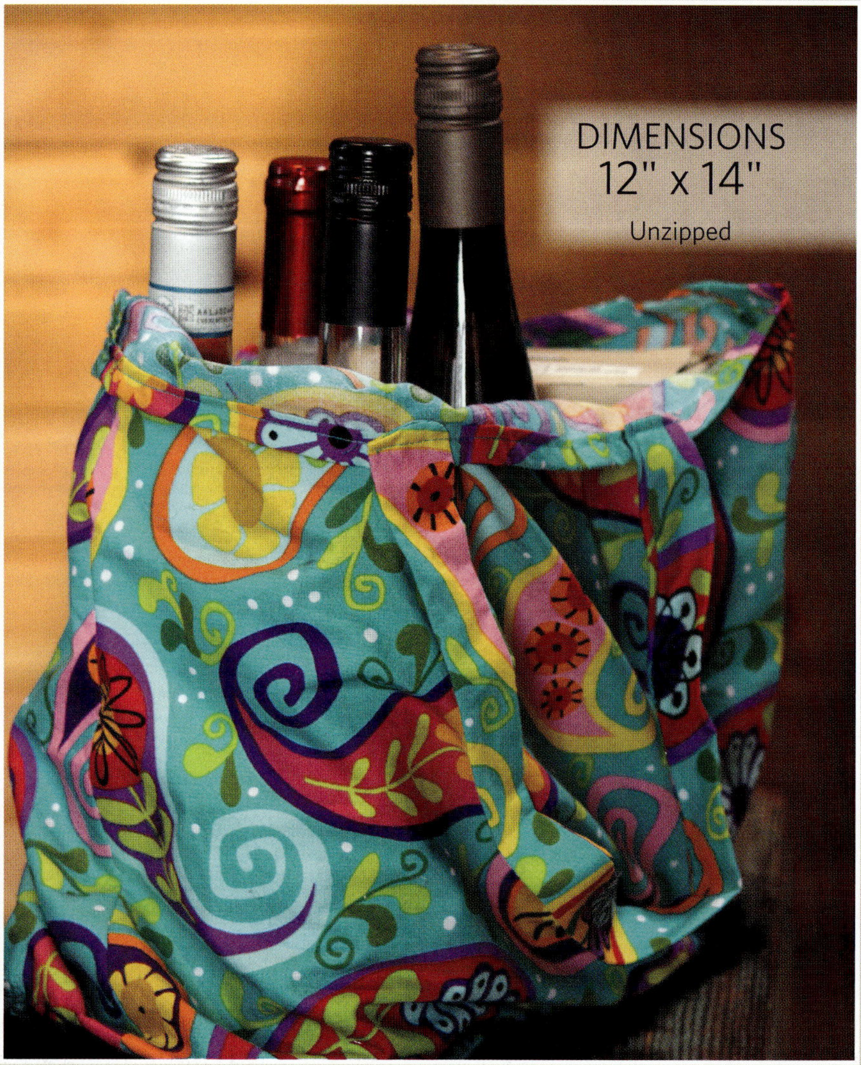

IT HAPPENS EVERY TIME I GO ON A TRIP AND I BET IT HAS HAPPENED TO YOU TOO. Despite good intentions to pack light for the much-needed vacation, and a firm resolution made under my breath not to buy anything while traveling . . . guess what? I find something to buy that I just can't resist.

Can you identify with this? The trouble is that because you were so frugal with your packing, you can't fit even an extra pack of postcards into your suitcase. So what do you do with that pile of treasures that won't fit into the suitcase even if an elephant were to sit on it while you attempt in vain to zip it up?

Never fear—you are prepared with your *Folk Art Flower Travel Tote*! When not in use, it zips up into a neat little package. When you are in need of a tote to carry home your treasures, just unzip it and you are all set.

Preparation:

1. Draw the pattern onto linen.
2. Select a yard of cotton fabric that will coordinate with the colors in the hooked part of the tote. Choose an 18" zipper that coordinates with the selected fabric.
3. Cut out two 19" x 18 ½" rectangles of the cotton fabric for the tote, and two 19" by 3" strips for the handles.

Hooking:

1. Hook the design using #6 and #8 cuts.
2. Crocheted edge: Use a size C crochet hook to crochet an edge around the hooked portion. I used a single crochet on this bag.

MATERIALS

¼ yard of linen backing

1 notch of wool in black (a notch is 6" x 16")

1 notch of wool in light yellow orange

1 notch of wool in medium yellow orange

2 notches of wool in red orange

2 notches of wool in turquoise

1 notch of wool in green

Zipper—18"

1 yard of cotton or cotton blend fabric for lining

Sewing thread to match lining

Crochet yarn: I used black Erdel Shaggy, available from Let Nola Do It

Button thread to match crochet yarn

Size C crochet hook

Sewing needle

Pinking shears

Marking pen

Ruler

Construction:

1. Lay out the lining fabric with right sides together. Using a ½" seam, sew the 18½" edge, the 19" edge, and the other 18½" edge. Trim corners. Pink the seam to prevent unraveling. Turn right side out.
2. Turn ½" raw edge to the inside of cotton tote, press. Turn another ½" to the inside. Stitch down right below the top edge, and stitch again ⅜" from the top edge.
3. Fold the handles in half lengthwise. Using a ¼" seam, sew the length of the handle, and along one short end. Turn the handle right side out and press. Do the same with the other handle. Tuck the raw ends of the handles about ¼" to the inside, and press. Sew the handles to each side of the tote, centering them, and leaving a 4½" space between each side of each handle.
4. Hand stitch the zipper in with button thread on the wrong side of the hooking, right next to the crocheted edge.
5. Turn tote right side out.
6. Flatten out the bottom, creating a point at each side. Mark a line perpendicular to the bottom seam that is 6½" across. Sew across the triangle formed. Repeat on the other side.
7. Hand stitch the bottom of the cotton tote to the back side of the hooked portion. Use a heavy duty matching thread and stitch it securely with a blind stitch or a whip stitch.
8. When it is not full of your treasures, fold the tote up, tuck it inside the hooked bottom, and zip it up for handy storage.

See pattern on page 98.

DEFINITELY DENIM "POCKET" POCKETBOOK

Designed, hooked, and constructed by Jennifer O'Malley

JUST LIKE A FAVORITE PAIR OF SHOES OR SLIPPERS, DENIM BLUE JEANS ARE LIKE AN OLD FRIEND. THIS IS WHY I LOVE TO REPURPOSE (OR UPCYCLE) DENIM INTO FUN, FUNCTIONAL ITEMS. One of the best qualities of denim is that it is strong, like leather. You may have seen fabric bags with leather bottoms—strength and durability where it is needed. That got me thinking about swapping the leather/fabric combo for denim and hooking. What a great way to marry my denim friends with my other favorite friend—wool. After you make this versatile bag, you will love the compliments coming your way in every grocery checkout line, banking or post office line, and, of course, at rug hooking events.

A conversation about color

I don't know about you, but when I was a kid nothing made me happier than a brand new box of crayons. To this day I surround myself with color at every opportunity. My home is full of color. My dishes are a full rainbow of Fiestaware. My closet, my wool stash, and even my sock drawers are full of assorted colors. It doesn't matter how large my wool stash is—I still cave in and buy more wool because I have to have "that color." Sound familiar? The more wool you buy, the more you hook; the more you hook, the more you cut; and what isn't hooked goes in the basket for that unplanned project down the road. We all have small mountains of already-cut worms, just waiting for a project.

And this is the perfect project. Choosing colors is a pleasure because denim goes with everything. I used everything that pleased my eye as I went along with no pre-planning, just deciding as I went.

Enjoy your *Definitely Denim "Pocket" Pocketbook*: denim and wool—it's the perfect marriage of durability and wearable art!

MATERIALS

Seam ripper

Sharp fabric scissors

Sewing machine with durable sewing machine needle suitable for denim, and zipper foot

Pinking shears for trimming (optional)

A basketball-size mound of wool worms.
- Cut size should be consistent. I used mostly #6 cut.

4 back pockets from adult blue jeans

2 waistbands from adult size blue jeans, including front buttons, cut to 26" (for shoulder straps)

5" piece of waistband, including buttonhole (for closure strap)

3" x 27" piece of denim (for top of hooked piece)

4" x 27" piece of denim (for bottom of hooked piece)

Tight linen or rug warp for hooking: 11" x 27" with edges serged or securely zigzagged to prevent fraying

10" x 27" piece of flannel (for lining)

2 pieces of lining cut to 4" x 11" (for matching insert)

Strong blue thread to match your denim

Strong gold thread (for topstitching)

Strong thread for adding buttons, for sewing hooked seam, and sewing on Velcro dots

1 Velcro dots (for flap pocket closure)

2 metal buttons (for flap pocket and closure strap)

1 nylon knee-high stocking (to secure work to hooking frame)

1 piece of thin cardboard ($2\frac{1}{2}$" x $9\frac{1}{2}$") for interior bottom insert

Preparation

You should start with a good quality seam ripper. Pace yourself on this part of the process because this will tire your hands. Denim jeans are durable, so don't be surprised if you break your seam ripper in the process. It's always a good idea to have a spare ripper on hand, just in case.

A word of caution: Follow my instructions and trim away multiple layers of cloth to minimize stress on your sewing machine.

1. Start by removing the 4 back pockets.

2. Peel back the corner seams of pockets, and trim excess layers, if needed.

3. Cut off the waistbands.

4. Use your seam ripper to remove the remaining belt loops.

5. Run your seam ripper through the lower edge of the waistband.

6. Remove middle layer of the waistband.

7. Remove the loose threads as you go.

8. Topstitch with a strong gold thread to replace what you ripped away.

Adding pockets

I designed this to include both open pockets and pockets with flaps. The open pocket is great if you are addicted to lip gloss and have to get to it quickly. The pocket with the flap will secure a cell phone or keys.

1. Position one pocket wrong side up. Place another pocket on top with right side facing up. Place Velcro dot pieces in place, test that the flaps will close, then hand sew the dots in place.

2. Fold flap down and sew metal button on as shown. Pin the two pockets together.

3. Trim excess denim from the sides.

4. Draw a center line in the middle of the backing and 1" from left and right edge. Your hooking will be 1" from the side edges. Position both pockets on backing as shown. With the flap up, topstitch with gold thread just on the bottom part of the pocket, to secure the pocket to the backing. Repeat this step for the open pocket on the right.

5. Allowing 1" seam allowance, stitch the 3" x 27" piece of denim, right side facing down, to the top of the backing material. Stitch the 4" x 27" piece of denim right side down to the bottom of the backing.

6. Stitch again ¼" out, then zigzag in between those rows of stitching. This is important since you will be stretching the denim and the backing over your hooking frame.

7. Stitch the top flap right above the open part of the pocket to secure.

8. With right side of lining facing up, position the last pocket (right side up) in the center of the right half of the lining. Pin it in place, and sew where original topstitching was on the pocket sides and bottom.

Secure the backing to your hooking frame

This technique will save you from stitching extra fabric to the sides of your backing. You will find this step allows more room to hook up to the drawn edge. I credit this tip to a member of my rug hooking guild. Thanks Alma!

1. Cut nylon knee high stocking into 6 strips, each ½" wide.

2. Using your hook, pull a loop through your backing.

3. Thread the loop through the larger open end and pull to tighten.

4. Now you can stretch your backing to your frame and work up to the drawn edge.

Hide your hooked seam

This technique will disguise where your side seam starts or stops.

1. Create random lengths of loose wool on the starting edge and leave them there for now. Vary the colors and use lengths that please you. I suggest that you add a row of textured wool occasionally so that the hooking does not look like a roll of candy lifesavers.

2. Hook right up to the pocket. Don't bring up the tail on the vertical edge of the pocket; bring tails up on the slanted bottom pocket edge to make a nice crisp edge.

3. When you approach the end of a row, trim a few tails from the beginning of the row that you started, and finish hooking with that same wool.

4. Bring the starting edge close to the ending edge to be sure your colors are the same and that they match up.

5. When the hooked section is complete, pinch the sides of your hooking together, tucking in the raw edges. Hand sew with strong quilting thread or waxed thread; stitch between the loops.

6. Your seam should be well hidden.

Assemble the lining

1. Fold the lining fabric in half, right sides together. Stitch a 1" seam allowance on the right and bottom edges, leaving a large enough opening to turn the pocketbook inside out. Backstitch close to the opening.

2. With pinking shears, trim to about ¼".

3. Pulling the layers apart on both bottom corners, shape into an even triangle.

4. Draw a stitching line 1 ½"from the outside tip; pin and stitch.

5. Trim to ¼". This gives the pocketbook a nice rectangular shape on the bottom.

6. Turn lining right side out.

7. Change to a zipper foot. Pin and stitch a 1" seam on the denim bottom section.

8. Pin and stitch a 1" seam on the denim top section.

9. Stitch the entire side seam again to reinforce, still using your zipper foot. Repeat steps 3 – 5 for same rectangular shape on the bottom.

Add lining and straps

1. Slip the lining inside the denim/hooked piece with right side of the hooking facing the right side of the lining.

2. Match up seams of both pieces and smooth out the inside area the best you can.

3. With button side facing up, place the shoulder strap between the lining and the hooked side. Each end should be about 1½" from outside edge, and center part of the strap toward the bottom of the bag. With right side of buttonhole piece (cleaner stitching faced down), slip the closure strap buttonhole in first and center between the straps. Pin in place.

4. Smooth out remaining edges and pin.

5. Stitch ½" seam allowance along the entire top edge, reinforcing straps and closure straps by backstitching. No need to trim this seam.

6. Reach through opening in the lining and carefully pull the straps through.

7. Tucking the hooked part into a ball, carefully work it through the opening.

8. Gently pull the bottom of the lining, and fold under the edges of the lining.

9. Topstitch the opening closed. This will be hidden by the insert piece, which you will construct next.

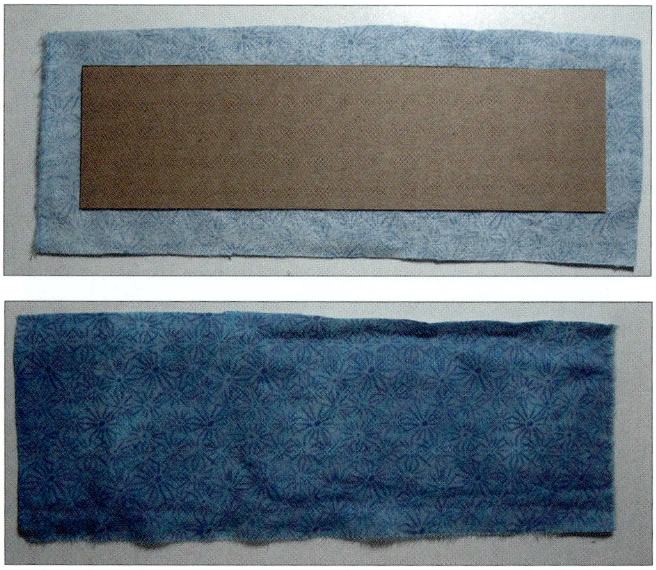

10. Create the cardboard insert. Sandwich the cardboard between 2 remaining pieces of lining, right sides of lining facing out.

11. Using your zipper foot, straight stitch just missing the cardboard. Center and smooth as you go.

12. With pinking shears, trim away the excess material. Smooth the lining to the inside and snuggle the insert to the bottom of the pocketbook.

13. The insert allows the bottom to lay flat and adds stability to the pocketbook.

14. Using your gold thread, evenly topstitch the top edge of the pocketbook. (Note: Photo shows shoulder strap, not to be confused with the closure strap.)

15. Closure strap: Sew the metal button right on the seam of the hooking and denim.

HOOT OWL HANDBAG

Designed, hooked, and constructed by Norma Batastini

MATERIALS

Linen backing

Wool: #4- and 5-cut strips

- Selection of 10 overdyed solids and textures
- Tan texture, off-the-bolt (for the owl body)
- Two different turquoise wools: 1/8 yd. of each (for the background)
- 1/16 yd. of each of the other colors, or a strip about 5" x 16"
- Dark brown plaid: a few strips
- Dark green plaid: a few strips

Cotton fabric for lining: 20" x 36"

50" leather strap (Mautto Fine Handbags and Straps, *www.mautto.com*)

O-rings (Mautto Fine Handbags and Straps, *www.mautto.com*)

Folk Art Style

A MOLA IS A PANEL USED IN THE CONSTRUCTION OF THE TRADITIONAL BLOUSES OF THE KUNA INDIANS OF PANAMA. A mola consists of several layers of different colored cotton fabric, each about 10" x 14", basted together like a sandwich. Using a reverse appliqué technique, the design is formed by cutting away part of each layer to expose the fabric below. Two panels—front and back—with the addition of a yoke and sleeves are used to construct a blouse. The Kuna have been making molas since the late 1800s and they are now a collectible form of folk art.

The design elements and styles of molas are perfect for rug hooking. Favorite motifs of the Kuna include the flora and fauna of the San Blas Islands—turtles, lizards, birds, leaves, seeds, and flowers. To replicate the effect of the layers of cotton found in real molas, rug hookers add a series of outlines that can be hooked with different colors. Backgrounds can be filled with many shapes, including labyrinths, slits, triangles, or squares. The number of outlines used and the concentration of fillers contribute to the look of a real mola. (For more information on rug designs based on molas see the article "Magnificent Molas," November/December 2011 issue of *Rug Hooking* magazine.)

For this handbag design, I chose an owl motif. Owl designs are popular in textiles, clothing patterns, and home décor. The simple owl shape lends itself well to the mola techniques of outlining and filling. The owl body and wings are outlined with gold, reddish brown, and orange. The entire owl is outlined with bright teal. The body of the owl features curved shapes as "fillers" that give the illusion of feathers. The leaf shapes balance the owl shape and add to the tropical theme. The leaves are also outlined. "Fillers," which use up or fill the background area, can be small florets or slits. The front and back of the handbag are the same design, reversed. In Kuna culture, duality is a recurring theme and often their molas repeat designs. The bottom of the bag is a solid band of color.

Choosing Colors and Fabrics

The colors used in real molas are bright. Intense reds, oranges, and golds are often placed against a red, blue, or black background for maximum contrast. For this handbag, I chose two turquoise blues for the background: one a mottled solid and one an overdyed texture. The solid was slightly brighter and I used it to outline the entire perimeter of the handbag and the main motifs. This gave a glow to the motifs and set them off from the rest of the background. The texture was used for most of the background, with the solid mixed in throughout for variety and depth.

Owl: I worked with a palette of tan, gold, orange, and red-orange that complements the turquoise blues. The tan body of the owl is a texture, giving a feathery look. Accents on the body are gold, orange, and fuchsia. The gold outline sets off the head and wings. The eyes are highlighted with gold, giving this bird a wide-eyed look. The beak, pupils, and talons are hooked with a dark brown plaid.

Leaves and branch: The lower leaf is hooked in solid khaki green with multicolor accents. The upper leaf is hooked with a spot-dye green and fuchsia accents. The branch the owl is perched on is hooked with the spot-dye green. The leaves and the branch are set off with a dark green plaid. One row of plaid outlines the upper leaf, the center vein, the bottom leaf, and the lower side of the branch. This dark accent balances the dark brown plaid used in the owl.

Background details: Scattered on the background are small florets and lines or slits of colors.

Tips for fine hooking with textures

1. Consider using #4- and 5-cut textures to add interest to detailed hooking.
2. Choose textures carefully. Use only textures that are tightly woven. Many textures have a tight weave and will not fray when cut.
3. Look for wool in vintage clothing. Recycled women's clothing is often made of wool that is a tight weave and comes in colors and plaids not available today.
4. When cutting a texture, be careful to stay on the straight of the grain. Cut parallel to the selvedge for a stronger strip.
5. Cut a texture one size up. For instance, if you are using #4-cut solid strips, cut your textures in a #5 cut. The softer edges of the texture will melt into the hooking and appear as a #4 cut.

Using the same colors over and over is a technique to balance color, value, and intensity. The slits in each area are all hooked with one color. This is a technique found in molas: leftover fabric scraps are slipped between layers to add more color in a small area.

Bottom: The bottom of the bag was hooked with a reddish-brown check.

Hooking

1. Outlining is important when hooking in the mola style. The outlines of each section of the owl were hooked first and the whole owl was outlined with solid turquoise. All of this outlining sets up the shape of the head, body, and wings.
2. Hook the eyes, beak, and talons.
3. Then hook the accents.
4. Finally, the body, wing, and head shapes were filled in.
5. Now hook the leaves. Each leaf was outlined with an orange and a tan and then a row of the solid turquoise. The accents within each leaf were hooked after the outline, and finally the body of each leaf was filled in.
6. Outline the small florets with one color and fill in the shape with another. A few loops of green were used for the centers and a small leaf. The florets were partially outlined with solid turquoise. The partial outlining was sometimes for artistic value and sometimes for practicality. There may not have been space to fit the row all around the floret.
7. Hook the entire perimeter of the front and back of the bag with solid turquoise. Around each motif, hook a row of textured turquoise next to a row of the solid turquoise. The contrast between the two turquoise wools highlights the motifs and pops them out.
8. Hook the rest of the background in a mix of the two turquoise wools.
9. Hook the bottom of the bag in straight rows with an overdyed check. This check coordinates with the dark reddish browns in the owl.

Hooking the Owl Eyes

1. First eye: Hook the smallest circle first with orange wool and count the loops needed to hook around all the way. I used 12–13 loops, plus ends.
2. Hook the second eye with the orange wool, using the same number of loops. This keeps the eyes the same size. (When hooking circles or other shapes which you want to be evenly sized, count the stitches to keep them approximately the same.)
3. Hook the next row with gold, very close to the orange wool.
4. Hook the next row with reddish-brown wool, close to the gold wool.
5. Fill in the center (pupil) with dark brown plaid.
6. Add the highlight with cotton or linen thread. Using a tapestry needle, stitch the highlight in from the back of the piece. Cut ends and knot the linen in the back. A thread of linen or cotton will last longer than a piece of fine-cut white wool that will fray and disappear over time. (Hint: Save threads of linen, monk's cloth, or rug warp when cutting off excess backing in your projects. Keep them in your tool bag for times when you need a highlight.)

Construct the bag

Assembling the bag

When the hooking is completed, steam the pieces, both front and back, and let them dry. Zigzag or secure the backing about 1" from the hooking. Cut off the excess backing. Press the 1" of backing to the back of the hooking. Using a heavy double thread, sew together the sides of the handbag. I used a ladder stitch, working on the right side of the handbag. Reinforce with several stitches at the top and the bottom of the seam. Press the 1" of backing along the top of the handbag into the back. Gently baste the backing to the hooking, all along the top inside edge. Along the sides, where the top backing meets the backing of the side seams, reinforce those points with additional stitches.

Attach the O-rings inside each side of the handbag. The O-ring sits half above the top of the bag and half below. Stitch the rings securely to the backing, along the bottom half of the ring.

Lining

Choosing a lining is a great way to enhance the colors used in your handbag. I chose a rust-colored geometric cotton quilting fabric. Satins, silks, and other smooth fabrics would also work well. Cut one piece of fabric about 2" larger than the finished hooked pieces, approximately 14" x 20". Measure your finished handbag before you cut, as sizes can change during hooking. You will need at least 1" extra all around for seam allowance and adjustments.

If you would like pockets inside, now is the time to add them. Cut another piece of fabric about 14" x 10". Fold it in half lengthwise, and place it onto one side of the lining piece. The folded edge of the panel should be placed near the top. Turn under the bottom edge of the panel and stitch it to the lining piece. Open up and determine where to stitch to form the pockets. I placed my cell phone in the space to determine the size. Stitch vertically to form the pocket.

Next, fold the lining piece right sides together, and stitch the sides. The panel will be secure within the side seams. Slip the lining into the handbag to check the size. Fold the top edges of the lining down to meet the top of the hooking. Make adjustments as needed, then press.

Stitch the corners of the lining into the corners of the hooking. My stitches went through the backing, where I made a few stitches between the loops. Carefully stitch the lining to the top of the bag. I used a dark brown Valdani pearl cotton thread. Make tiny stitches, going in between every hooked loop to pull the lining up close to the hooking.

Handles and Magnetic Closure

Stitch carefully around the O-rings. If any of the backing is exposed, cover it with stitches of the dark brown thread.

Now add a magnetic closure. Measure along the top of the handbag to find the exact center. Place the closure inside, on the lining, about ½ inch from the top. Sew the closure on by going through the lining and through the hooking to the outside of the handbag. Guide the needle back through to the inside, hiding the stitches between loops. Continue stitching until the closure is secure. Sew the other side of the closure to the opposite side of the bag, carefully aligned so that they match and close naturally.

Attach the leather strap hook to the O-rings with the attached clip.

See pattern on page 99.

"TWO FOR ONE" MARKET BAG

Designed, hooked, and constructed by Sharon A. Smith

DIMENSIONS

11" x 18" x 16"

11" (bottom width) x 18" (top width) x 16" (height)

THIS DELIGHTFUL TWO-SIDED TOTE OFFERS ENDLESS DESIGN POSSIBILITIES. Hook the same motif on both sides of the bag or have different images for the front and back. Either way, this market bag will surely bring smiles to you and others. My piece features shoppers on one side—we are all familiar with these crazed, shopping-frenzied women, aren't we? The other side is a menagerie of primitive animals. Make this bag your own—and make a statement!

MATERIALS

Wool: about 2 yds. in various colors

Linen thread or worsted weight yarn

Darning needle (or other wide-eyed needle)

Lining: ½ yd. lining material

Handles: 24" leather

Preparation

Transfer the pattern to the linen. You will see that this is hooked in three separate pieces. You might think it would be quicker to combine some of the pieces and hook them together, as one larger piece, but that is not the best way to proceed for this type of market bag. Hooking it in three pieces allows for sturdier, 90-degree angle edges on the finished market bag. If you hook it all as one piece (that is, the bottom panel and the front together in one piece), the folded edges will be rounder and it will lose the shape you want. This may seem like more work, but the finished product will be better.

Hooking

1. Begin by hooking all the edges; that way you have nice straight edges for ease in assembling.

2. The bottom of the bag is a great open space where you can add your own designs or your initials.
3. After the hooking is completed, trim off the extra linen, leaving about 1" of linen around each piece. Secure these edges using a zigzag stitch or other locking stitch on your sewing machine. Press.

Assemble the bag

Hand stitch the 3 pieces together. This allows for sturdier, 90-degree-angle edges.

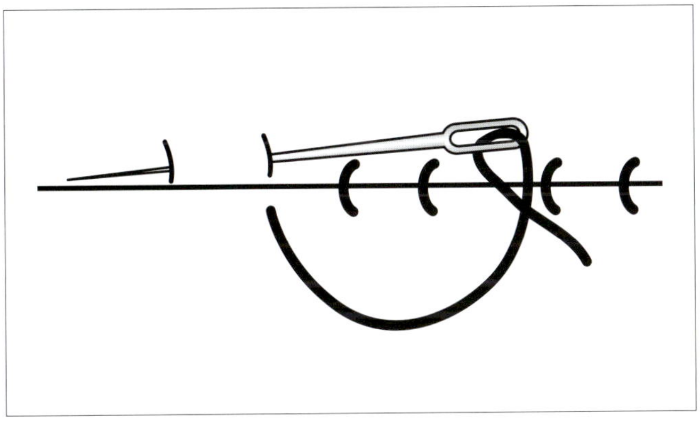

Method A: *Stitch with linen thread and an invisible slip stitch*

- From a scrap piece of linen, pull several strands of linen threads. Use these to stitch up the bag. You can wax the threads if you like to make it easier to stitch.
- Fold the raw linen edges inward and finger press.
- Hold the folded edges from both pieces together so that the finish hooked wool part is on the outside.
- Leaving a 3" tail, slip the threaded needle inside and out the fold of piece #1.
- Crossing directly across, place your needle in and out of the folded edge of piece #2.
- Continue going back and forth for about 3". Now take each end of the thread in your left and right hand and pull tightly without breaking the thread. This should bring the bag pieces close together and hide the edging even more.
- Continue in this manner until the end of the seam. Go back and tie a knot in the end and hide the tail.

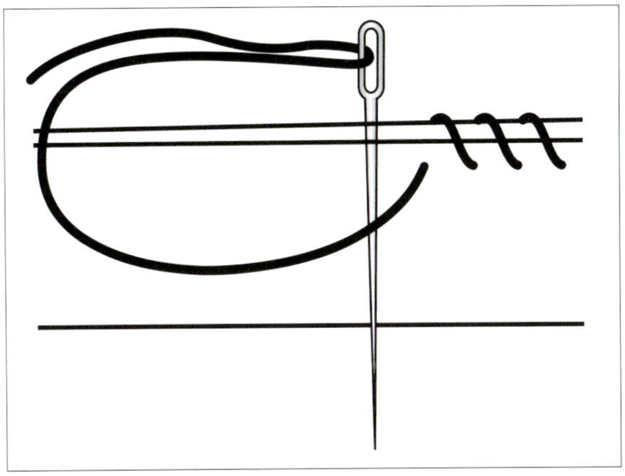

Method B: *Whip stitch with yarn*

- Use worsted weight rug yarn or other strong wool yarn.
- Thread a darning needle with the strong yarn, knot one end.
- Put your needle into one edge of one hooked piece. Pull it up and place needle over into the other edge of the other bag piece.
- Pull the yarn snug against the linen. Don't pull too tight or the edge will buckle.
- Bring your needle around the top of the two edges, and insert the needle back into the first hooked piece.
- Continue whipping along the raw edges, careful to cover all the linen.

Optional: *add a rigid bottom support piece*

If you want to add some structure to the bag, consider adding a rigid support piece to the bottom of the bag. Cut a piece of sturdy cardboard, plastic, or a thin board to fit snuggly into the bottom of the bag. Place the rigid piece inside for added reinforcement and strength. This will be between the hooked piece and the lining.

Lining

1. Cut pieces of lining fabric:
   - » 2 pieces 15" x 17" for front and back
   - » 1 piece 4" x 10" for the bottom

2. If you want interior pockets, sew them on now.

3. With right sides together, machine sew the front lining panel to the back panel. Either hand stitch or machine sew the bottom panel of the lining to the sides of the lining. If you are adding the optional rigid bottom, insert it now.

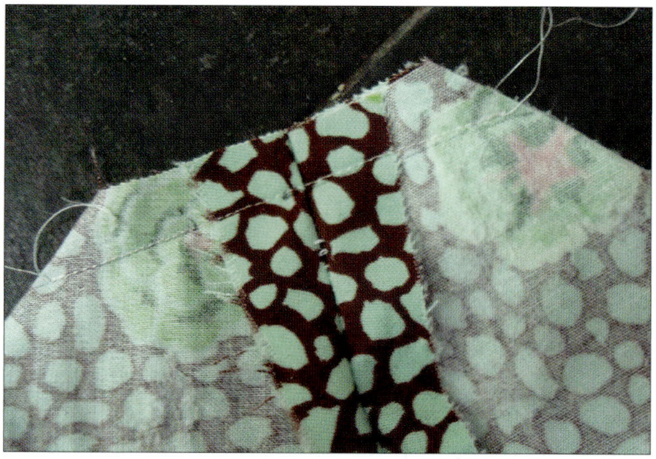

4. Fold the bottom panel and side seam to form a triangle. Draw a straight line 2" from the point, across the open seam, from one edge to the other edge. Sew on this line, and cut off the excess fabric on the corner.
5. Leave the lining pouch inside out. Now slip it into the hooked bag. Carefully tug and push the lining into place until it fits snugly. You may have to adjust the lining seams so that they match the seams in the hooked bag and fit well.
6. Fold under the top raw edge of the top of the lining. Pin it to the inside of your bag, between the lining and the hooked section. Hand stitch the lining to the bag all around the top edge.

Yo-yo Embellishment

The simplest way to make yo-yos is to use Clover's Quick Yo-Yo Maker. The little tool, priced about $5 to $8, is well worth the price. It comes in three sizes, to make three different size yo-yos.

- » Size ¾" makes an extra small yo-yo
- » Size 1¼" makes a small yo-yo
- » Size 1¾" makes a large yo-yo

Easy directions come with the tools. The yo-yos used in this bag are the small size at 1¼".

Make the yo-yos in cotton fabrics to complement the lining. Hand sew each one onto the lining separately, stitching several places through the back of the yo-yo. Another option is to find ready-made yo-yos. Sometimes they can be found on Etsy or in craft stores. I used about 20 yo-yos for this bag.

Handles

Hand stitch the handles to the outside of the bag. Use a simple securing stitch on the leather tabs. Shown here are the inside and the outside of the handle attachments.

See patterns on pages 100–101

EAST WEST CLUTCH

Designed, hooked, and constructed by Cindy Irwin

DIMENSIONS
16" x 7"

MATERIALS

Backing: I use linen backing. It's a little stiffer than cotton backing, so it adds a little more body.

Wool:

- $^1/_2$–$^3/_4$ yd., depending on how high you hook and how much you pack
- (1) 8-value swatch

Antique buttons

Thread: Furrier Waxed or any strong thread

16" separating jacket or purse zipper

Purse feet

Plastic needlepoint canvas

Lining fabric: 18" x 24"

Handle: choose the handle color before the purse color. You can always dye wool to match the handle if you want it to match. There are many sites online where you can buy handles.

YOU WILL NEVER LOSE YOUR KEYS IN THIS BAG! It's long, shallow design makes it easy to keep everything organized and at your fingertips.

Preparation

1. Transfer the pattern to the backing. There are many ways to transfer your pattern to your backing. Pick the one you are the most comfortable with.

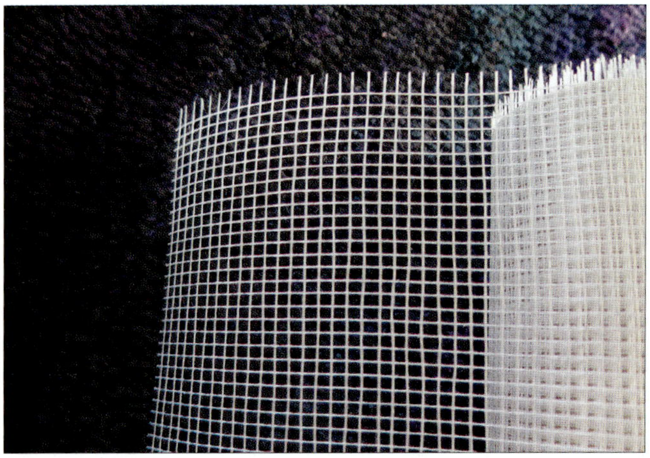

- I use Crack Stop to transfer small patterns. Crack Stop is a fiber grid that is sticky on one side; the open grid allows you to draw on it and have the lines appear on the layer below. Lay the Crack Stop on your paper pattern and trace the pattern onto the Crack Stop. Then lay the Crack Stop on your backing and trace the pattern onto your backing. Crack Stop can be purchased online.
- Or you can use a light box. I made a simple light box by putting lights beneath an old glass patio table.

2. Angle a pencil on the linen and draw a line keeping it in the groove of the linen. This will give you a straight line for the bottom of your pattern.

3. Position the pattern on the pencil line.

4. Trace the pattern.

5. Now attach the zipper. Draw a line ¼" from the top of your pattern. Use this line as a guide. Pin, baste, and then sew the zipper to the top of your pattern using the second line as a guide. The outside edge of the zipper should line up with the second line.

6. Take the zipper apart after you have it lined up on both sides. Pin, baste, and sew it in place. Notice this zipper is too long for the bag. After you put it together, you can tack the end and cut it off.

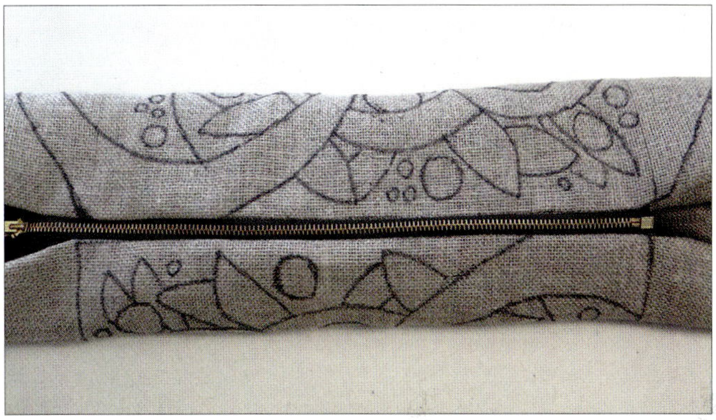

7. Zip the two sides together to make sure the sides of the pattern line up.

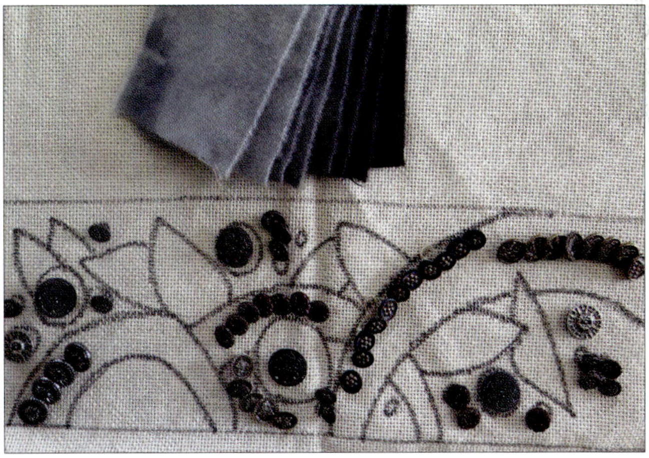

8. I used antique buttons to embellish this bag. It would look lovely with gemstones as well. Sew the buttons onto the backing.

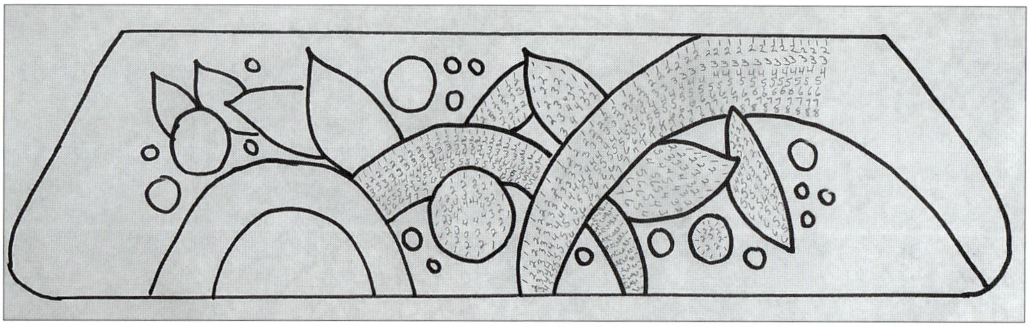

See this enlarged shading diagram on page 103.

Hooking

1. This bag was hooked with a gray 8-value swatch in a #3 cut. Look at the diagram of contour shading for hooking this piece. When you are contour shading, use every value in the swatch. Do not skip a value.

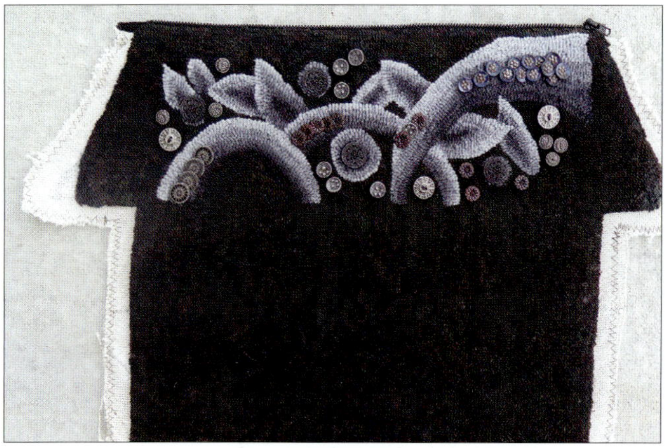

2. Hook the design on the back of the purse with your background wool. Use one cut larger than the rest of the background. It gives your bag another subtle point of interest.

Lining

Use your finished hooking for the lining pattern. Do not use the original pattern for the lining. Your hooked piece will grow and will be larger than the pattern.

Assembly

1. Serge or zigzag 1" around all sides of the hooking. Trim close to the stitching.
2. Steam lightly on the wrong side. If you have used buttons on the piece, be sure to use plenty of padding as you steam the piece.
3. Press the edge of the zipper to the inside.
4. Use the ladder stitch to sew seams together.

5. If the zipper you used does not exactly match the length of your hooking, you may have excess zipper on one side of the bag. Just zip the zipper, tack it at the edge of the bag, then cut off the extra length of zipper.

Hooking Hints

- When you hook along the zipper, hook close and tight so that the backing won't show.
- Hook perpendicular to the areas that will bend. This will keep the backing from showing through. If this isn't possible, pack the wool where the bag will bend.

LADDER STITCH INSTRUCTIONS

I learned this stitch from Kim Nixon, who taught me how to use it to put one of her stools together. It is a good way to sew two pieces together because the seam disappears.

1. Fold one panel edge in and lay that panel over the unfolded linen of the other panel. Butt the hooked sections together, and pin or baste in place.

2. Anchor the sewing thread on the backside of the hooked piece. Bring the needle up from the back, between the first and second row of hooked loops.

3. Take the needle down the other side, between vertical stitches and between the first and second row.

4. On the back, go up one stitch and take the needle through to the front, in between the first and second row of loops.

5. This is what the seam looks like on the back.

6. This is the front when the pieces are seamed together.

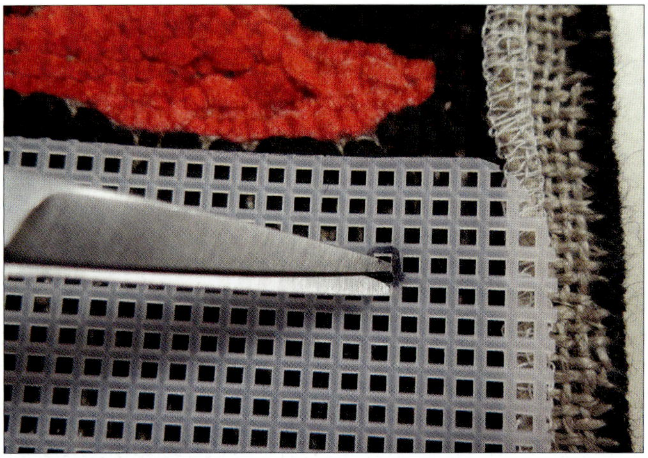

6. Cut needlepoint canvas to fit the bottom of bag. Round the corners. Mark the plastic canvas for feet. Snip the plastic canvas at marks, as shown.

7. Push each foot through the front of hooked piece. Do not cut backing, just wiggle the foot until it goes through the linen. Then push the foot through a hole in the plastic canvas.

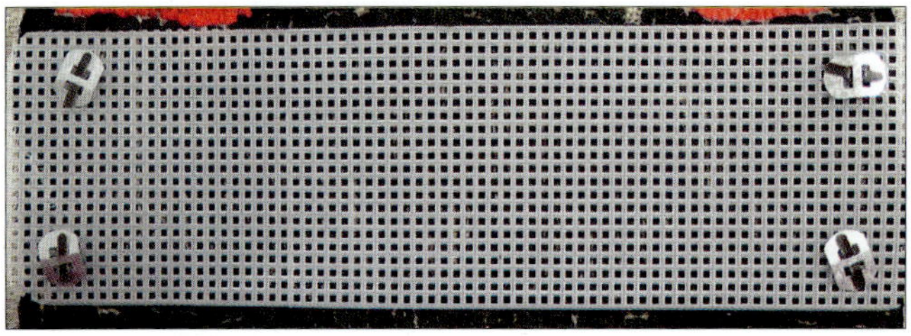

8. Place brackets over the feet and fold the prongs back.

Handles

Tack a piece of reinforcing material on the inside of the bag where you will attach the handles. Now sew handles onto your bag through this reinforcing material. You can use the plastic reinforcement material that you used for the bottom of the bag, but a heavy fabric will be easier to sew through. Artist canvas is the perfect weight. Sunbrella brand fabric is about the same weight as artist canvas.

See patterns on pages 102–103.

MILAN BAG

Designed, hooked, and constructed by Cindy Irwin

I SAW A BAG IN THIS STYLE BEING CARRIED BY A FRIEND AT A PARTY LAST YEAR. She told me she got it in Milan. I loved it so much that I convinced her to immediately dump out the contents into a paper bag so I could study it and use it as a pattern. (She agreed—she is a very good friend.) Since that party, I've seen this style many times, including in a vintage Chanel collection.

MATERIALS

Linen: 3/4 yd.

Wool: 1 to 1 1/2 yd.

Gemstones: Consider color, size, and luster when you pick gemstones. These gemstones work well in purse designs: onyx, pearls, lapis, jade, turquoise, jasper, crystals (with wool behind the crystals).

Wire

Crimp beads

Crimping tool

Wire snippers

Thread: Furrier Waxed thread, or any strong thread

1" grommets

Grommet tool

Purse feet

Plastic needlepoint canvas

Lining fabric: 1 yd.

Handle: 2 flat leather cords, 1/2" wide and 40" long. Choose the handle color before you choose the purse color. You can always dye the wool to match the handle. I use *allleathersupplies.etsy.com*

Preparation

1. For this bag, you will need four rectangles that are 9" high and 8" wide. Draw the pattern on the backing. To get a straight line on your backing, angle the pencil on the linen, and draw the line keeping the point of the pencil in one groove of the linen.
2. Position a grommet 1" from the top, carefully centered on each panel. Trace a circle around the grommet. Do not hook inside this marked grommet circle.
3. The bottom of the bag is 8" square. Be careful here: it is crucial that the bottom edges are the exact same measurement as the lower edges of the panels.

4. Draw your design on the linen, keeping the design away from the edges. It is easier to join the edges if there isn't a design to match.

The design on the red bag was inspired by mid-century modern design. For the blue bag, I played with pieces of lapis and jade until I liked the arrangement. My inspiration was a picture of a Frank Lloyd Wright design. I didn't copy his design, just used it for inspiration. Notice I forgot to draw the grommet circles. I had to adjust the patterns as I hooked them.

To add gemstones:

- When picking gemstones for your bag, consider the design. Think about where to place the stones: keep them away from the edges. Consider where you want sparkle and shine. And think about how hard the stones are.
- Arrange the gemstones on the backing—play around with the placement. Move them around until you are happy with the design. When you are satisfied, mark the location of each on the backing, then set them aside.
- Attach the gemstones with beading wire and crimp beads. Gemstones, even soft ones like pearls, have rough edges that will abrade thread. I once hand sewed 600 amethyst beads onto a bag only to have some of them fall off. Learn from my mistake and wire them onto your bag!
- If you use a large bead, wire it on, and when you are finished hooking, glue it to the backing for extra security. I use a product called Jewel Bond. It can be purchased at Fire Mountain Gems. (*www.firemountaingems.com.*)

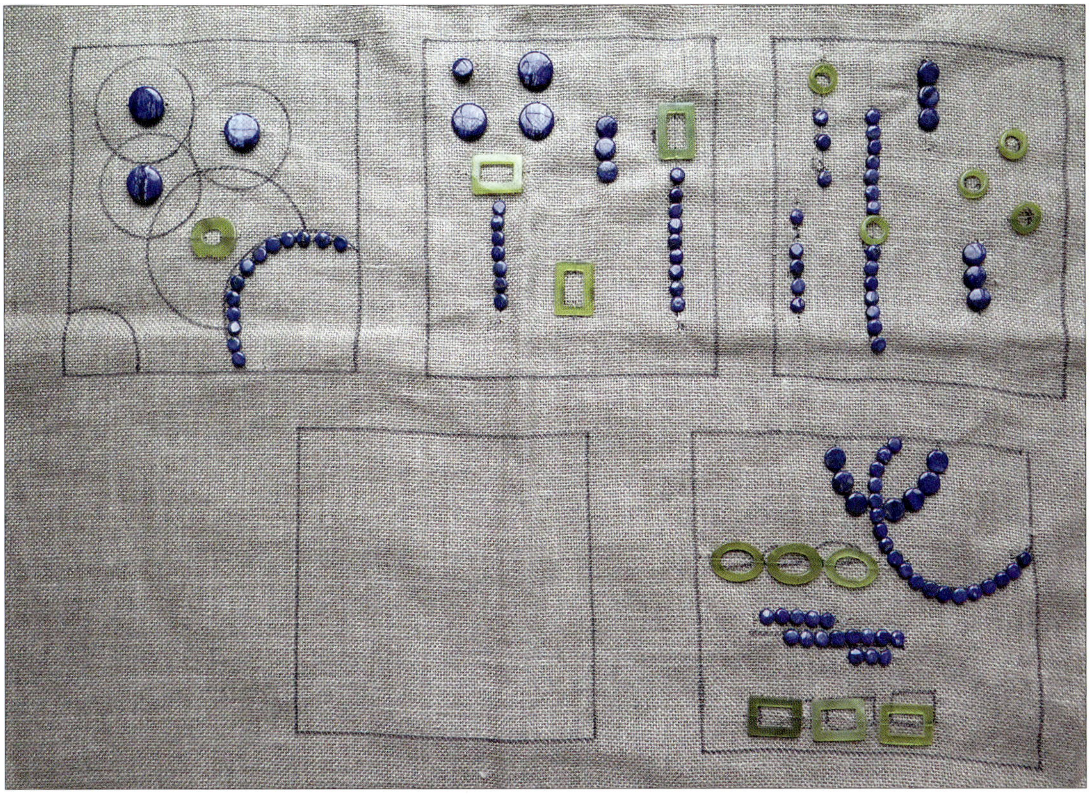

Move the beads and gemstones. around until you are pleased with the design.

Hook around the embellishments.

HOW TO ATTACH GEMSTONES

MATERIALS AND TOOLS

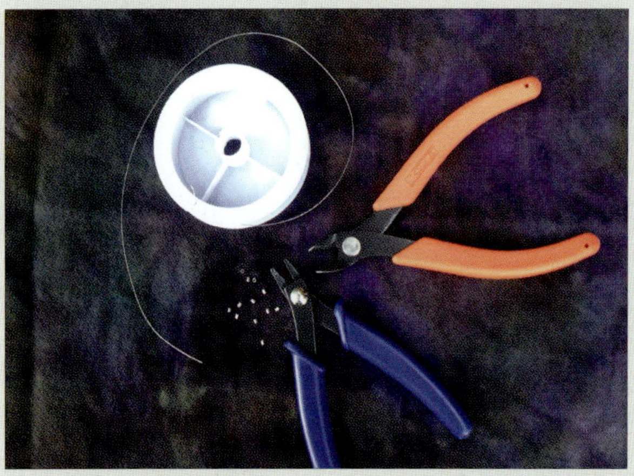

Wire
Crimp Beads
Crimper
Wire Cutter

If you are attaching one bead:

1. Run the wire through the bead, then through the backing. Make sure you insert the wire through the backing allowing at least 1/8" on either side. This will allow the bead to lie flat. If you insert the wire too close to the bead or under the bead, it won't lie flat.

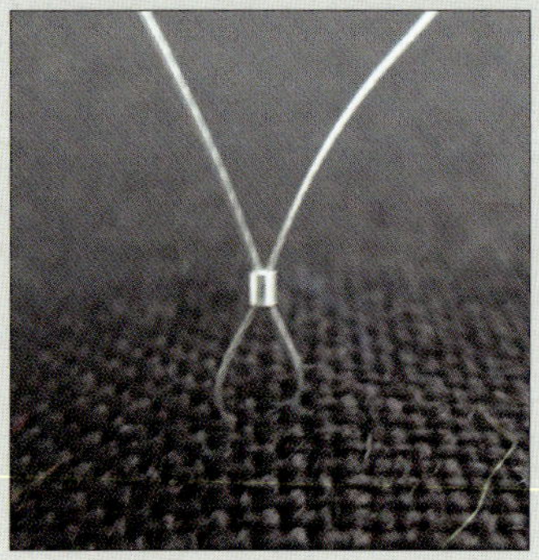

2. Take both ends of wire to the back of your pattern, then through a crimp bead.

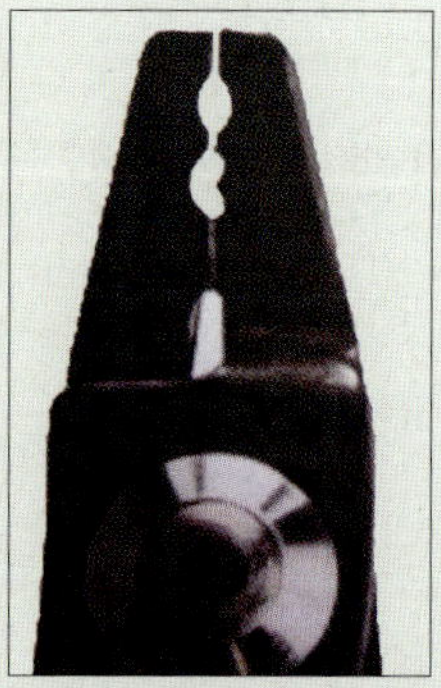

3. There are two holes on the crimping tool. The back one crimps or puts a divot in the crimp bead, the front hole rounds the crimp bead.

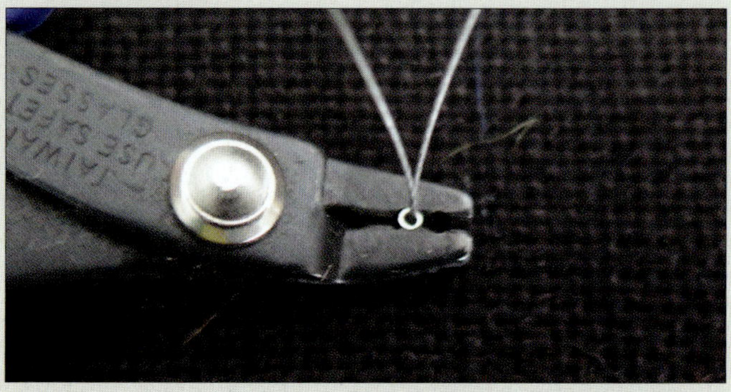

4. Position the crimp bead in the back hole. Pull up on the wires while pulling down on the crimp bead with the crimp tool.

5. Squeeze gently. This will create a divot in the crimp bead.

6. Turn crimp bead 90 degrees and crimp or bend the bead in half.

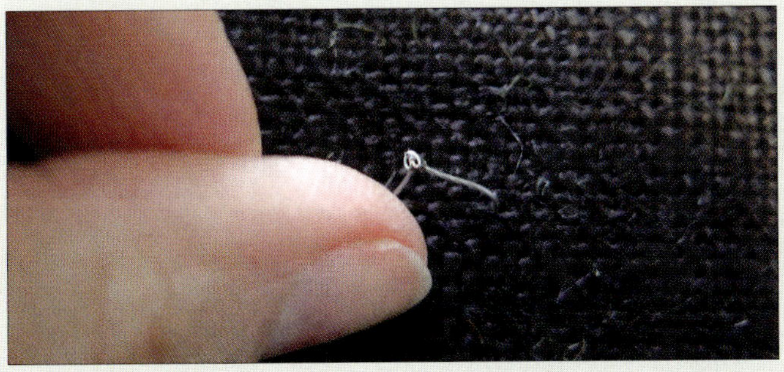

7. Clip excess wire off at the crimp bead.

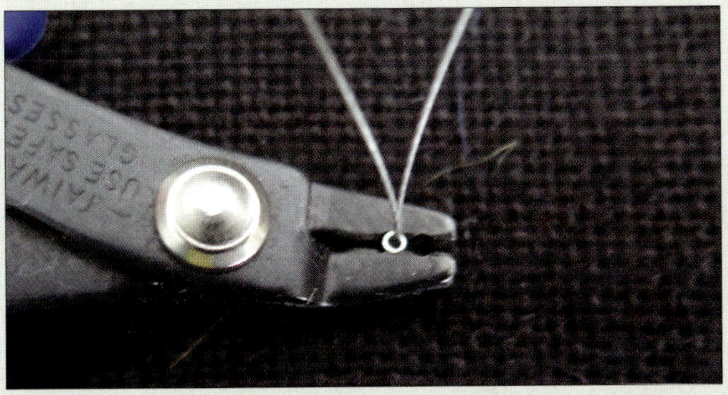

If you are attaching a row of beads:

1. Attach the wire to the backing. Do this by running both ends of the wire through the backing. Crimp.

2. Take the long end of the wire up through the backing, string the beads and take the wire through to the back.

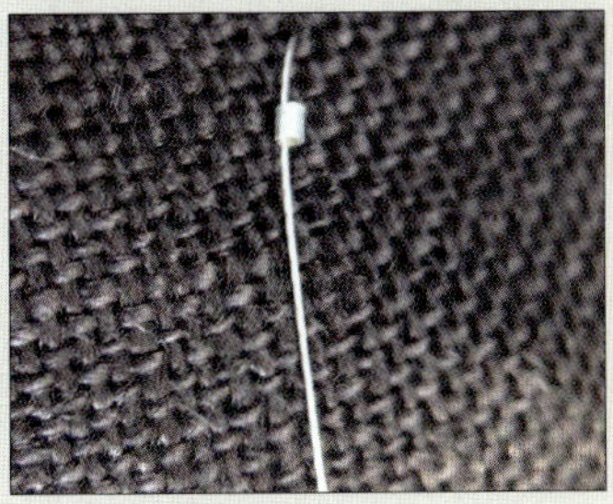

3. Insert the wire through a crimp bead.

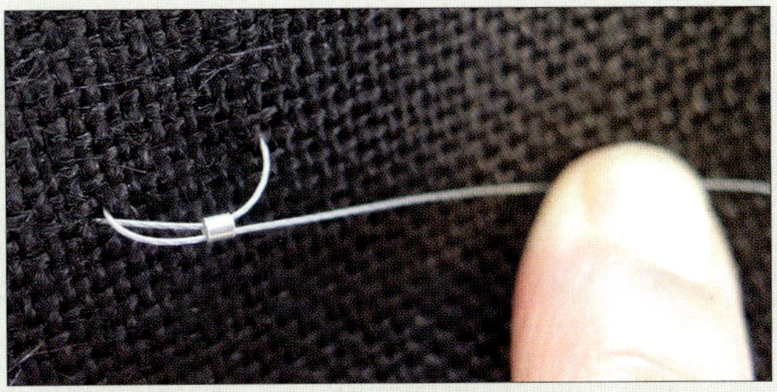

4. Take the wire up to the front, then take it back down about 1/4" from where you brought it up. Put the wire through the crimp bead, pull tight.

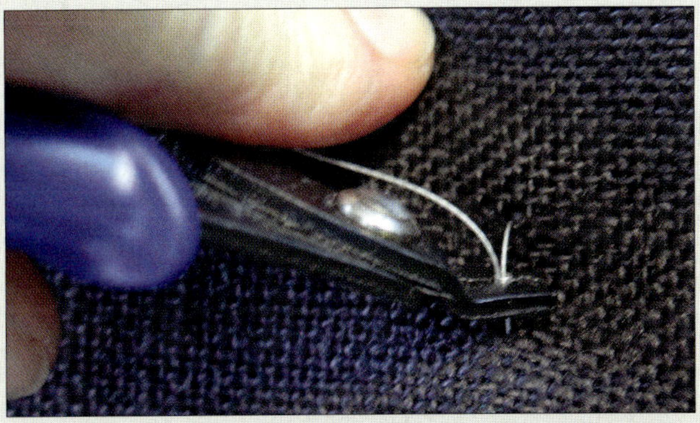

5. Crimp.

6. Sew the beads in place.

Hooking:

1. Hook loosely around the gemstones so they will lie flat. This is important: if you hook too tightly, it will interfere with the gemstones.
2. Hook perpendicular to the edges. This will keep the backing from showing. If it isn't possible to hook perpendicular, pack the wool around the edges of the linen.
3. When you are finished hooking, make sure the bottom edges are exactly the same length as the bottom edge of each panel. Adjust the bottom until everything matches.
4. Check and adjust the grommet circles. The top of the grommet should lie flat on the outside of the bag with no backing showing around the edges.
5. When the hooking is finished, serge or zigzag 2½" from the top of each panel, and ¾" around the other three sides of each panel. Serge ¾" around all four sides of the bottom panel. Cut close to stitching.

6. Sew the panels together using the ladder stitch. When the panels are sewn, check the folds. If you see linen at the fold, you may want to add another row of hooking where the bag bends.

Construction

1. Add the feet. Cut a piece of needlepoint canvas to fit bottom of bag. Round off the edges of this reinforcement piece. Now mark placement for the feet: for best results, place them ¾" from edge of canvas.

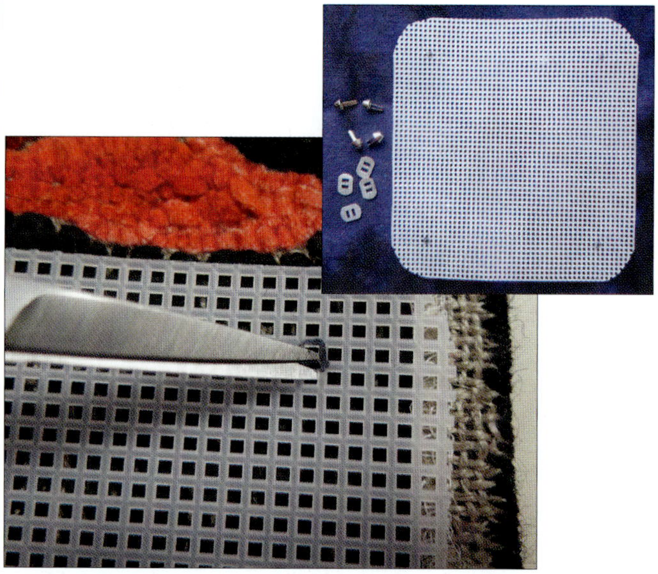

2. Snip plastic canvas. Push the foot through front of hooked piece. Do not cut backing, just wiggle the foot until it goes through the linen. Then push the foot through a hole in the canvas.

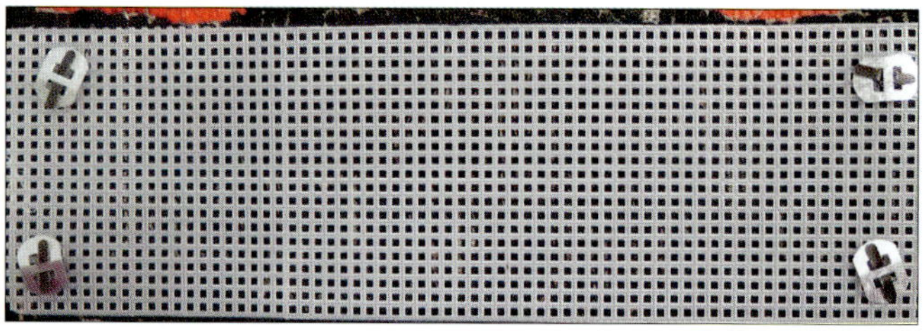

3. Place brackets over the feet and fold the prongs back.

Lining

There are a couple of options for linings. Sometimes I use the same wool for the lining that I used for the background. The advantage here is that it is easier to work with and will blend with the hooking. The disadvantage is that it will be a little bulky. If you use polished cotton or other fabric instead of wool, it won't be as bulky and will look more professional. I use both options, depending on the look I'm going for.

1. Measure for the lining before sewing your bag together. The lining should be the same size as the bag. Use the hooked panels as the pattern for the lining.
2. Reinforce the grommet holes. Cut a 2" x 2" piece of reinforcing fabric; I use plastic needlepoint canvas. Use a punching tool or a sharp pair of scissors to cut the hole in the reinforcing fabric. Be sure that the hole is the same size as the shank of the grommet.

3. Baste this reinforcement piece in place, on the inside of bag, centered on the grommet hole in your bag.
4. Insert the lining into the bag, wrong sides together, and sew around the top edge of the bag.

5. Attach the grommets. See the sidebar for instructions; there are also many YouTube videos on how to attach grommets.

INSERTING A GROMMET

There are many videos on YouTube that demonstrate how to attach grommets. Check them out for some great ideas. It is a good idea to practice a few times before you attach a grommet to your bag. This is how I insert a grommet.

MATERIALS AND TOOLS

You will need:

Grommets

Grommet tool

Hammer

Reinforcing material

1. As you hook, leave a circle of unhooked backing the same size as the grommet. Check to make sure the grommet fits before you begin to sew the bag together.

2. Lay the grommet over the circle and adjust your hooking. There should be no backing showing on the outside of the grommet.

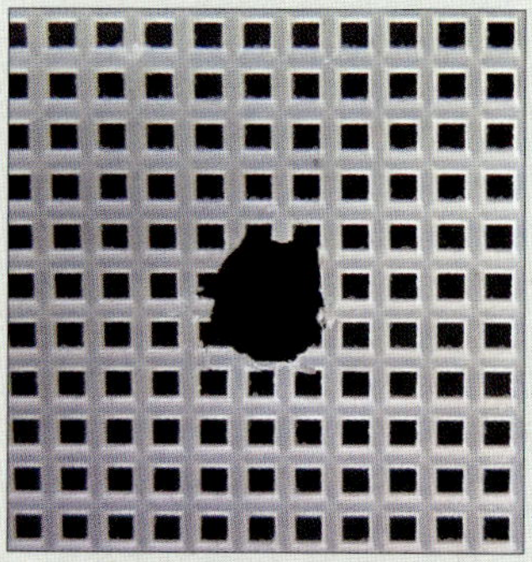

3. Remove the grommet. Cut a 2" x 2" piece of reinforcing fabric; I use plastic needlepoint canvas. With a punching tool or a sharp pair of scissors, cut a hole in the reinforcing fabric that is the same size as the shank of the grommet.

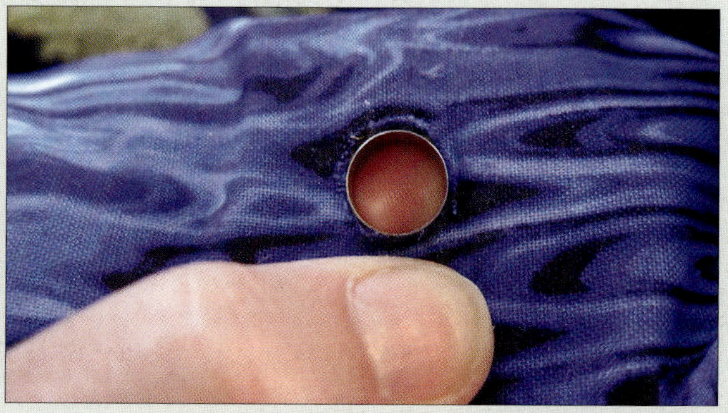

4. Tack the reinforcing fabric in place over the unhooked grommet hole on the inside of your bag. Cut a hole in your backing and lining that is the same size as the grommet shank. This can be done with the punching tool that often comes with your grommet kit, or you can cut the hole with a sharp pair of scissors.

5. From the front, place the shank through all layers: backing, reinforcing fabric, and lining.

6. Place the ring of the grommet over the shank.

7. Place the grommet over the base, insert setting tool, and strike with a hammer.

8. Finished grommet. If the grommet is correctly installed and tight enough, you should not be able to fit your fingernail under the grommet.

Handles

This purse requires two 40" soft leather cords for the handles. Thread each handle through two grommets that are opposite each other, and sew the ends together. Shown here are two different handle options.

See patterns on pages 104–105.

SUNFLOWER PURSE

Designed, hooked, and constructed by Cindy Irwin

HANDBAGS ARE GREAT FUN TO MAKE, BUT THERE ARE SOME TRICKS YOU NEED TO KNOW. One of the problems you face when assembling purses is sewing the hooked pieces together. It can be hard to accomplish this without having the backing show along the seam. Never fear—there are solutions! This bag avoids the difficulty altogether: it is made of a flat hooked panel with woolen sides.

See pattern on page 106.

Preparation

1. Transfer the pattern to the backing. There are many ways to do this. I like to use Crack Stop for small patterns. You can also use a light box. I use an old glass patio table with lights underneath.

MATERIALS

Backing: I use linen backing. It's a little stiffer than cotton backing; it adds a little more body.

Wool

- $\frac{1}{2}$–$\frac{3}{4}$ yd. background wool
- one 8-value swatch

Gemstones: These gemstones work well in purse designs: onyx, lapis, jade, crystals (if transparent, they will need wool lining under them), pearls (pearls are soft, but not brittle).

Wire

Crimp beads

Crimping tool

Wire snippers

Thread: Furrier Waxed or any strong thread

1" grommets and grommet tool

Purse feet

Magnetic closure

Plastic needlepoint canvas

Lining fabric:

- 17" x 16" piece of background wool
- two 5" x 7" pieces of background wool

Handle: Choose the handle color before the purse color. You can always dye the wool to match the handle. For this bag, you will need a flat leather cord $\frac{1}{2}$" wide and 65" long.

Optional: Crack Stop as an easy way to transfer small patterns. You can buy it online for about $30 for a 36" x 75' roll.

COLORS AND SHADING

1. I am lost without my color wheel. I knew I wanted turquoise beads and a red flower. The background is dark green wool overdyed with the primaries. I needed to pick a color for the space in between the beads.

2. I got out my color wheel and discovered that a split complementary plan with red, turquoise, and yellow green would work. I used a very dark value of yellow green for the inside of the flower. When hooked, it looks almost brown, but it is green. (I tried brown—it didn't work.)

4. This is a diagram of contour shading, or mock shading. The numbers in the petals correspond with the swatch numbers. *See a larger shading diagram on page 107.*

3. I used an 8-value swatch to hook the sunflowers. Make sure your 8-value swatch has a lot of contrast between the lightest value and the darkest value.

2. Add gemstones, if desired. (*See the sidebar on page 54 for directions*). Remember, do not pack the wool around your beads—if you do, they won't lie flat on the backing. If you use a large bead, wire it on; when you are finished with the hooking, also glue it to the backing. I use a product called Jewel Bond. It can be purchased at Fire Mountain Gems: *www.firemountaingems .com*
3. Be sure to mark the location of the grommets on the pattern.

Hooking

After the beads are attached, it's time to hook.

1. This bag is hooked in one main piece that bends along the bottom. The structure makes it easy to hook. This is what you need to know:
    - Hook perpendicular to the areas that will bend, i.e., the sides and bottom. This will keep the backing from showing through.
    - If this isn't possible, intentionally pack the wool where the bag bends.
    - Do not hook inside the grommet circles. When you are finished hooking, check and adjust each grommet circle. The top of the grommet should lie flat on the outside of the bag, with no backing showing around the edges.

2. I like to reproduce the pattern in a larger cut on the back of the bag using the background wool. It adds a subtle point of interest. Here I hooked in the shape of the sunflower that appears on the front of the bag.

Assembly

1. Serge or zigzag 1" around the hooking. Trim off the excess linen close to stitching. Steam and block. If you used gemstones in your design, steam lightly and carefully on the back of your hooking.

2. Fold edges of the linen to the back and bind the purse, using matching yarn. You want to have a very low-profile edge. Do not use cord.

Lining

1. You will need one 17" x 16" and two 5" x 7" pieces of background wool for your lining. You can use the same wool for the lining that you use for the background. The advantage to using wool is that it is easier to work with and will disappear. The disadvantage is that it will be a little bulky. If you use polished cotton or other fabric, it won't be as bulky and will look more professional.
2. Fold the 17" x 16" piece of fabric so that the 16" edge is at the top. Sew side seams with a ¼" seam allowance.

3. To make square corners:
    - Fold the side so that the seam is face up and it forms a triangle.
    - Measure up 2" from the point of the triangle on each side.
    - Mark a line, and sew on that line.
    - Trim bottom to ¼".
    - Do this on both sides.
    - Turn lining inside out.
    - Place 5" x 7" piece of wool over side seams.
    - The top should be even with top of lining. The bottom should be a little longer so you can fold it in.
    - Baste, then trim bottom edges.

Adding feet

1. Cut a piece of needlepoint plastic 3½" x 11". Tack the reinforcement plastic to the bottom of the bag. Mark where you want the feet to be.

2. Snip plastic canvas where marked for feet.

3. Push each foot through front of hooked piece. Do not cut the backing, just wiggle until it goes through the linen. Push the feet through holes in canvas.

4. Place brackets over feet and fold the prongs back.

5. Reinforce the grommet holes. Cut a 2" x 2" piece of reinforcing fabric. (I use plastic needlepoint canvas.) Use a punching tool or a sharp pair of scissors to cut a hole in the reinforcing fabric that is the same size as the shank of the grommet. Tack the reinforcing material to the inside of your bag so that the hole lines up with the grommet hole in your bag.

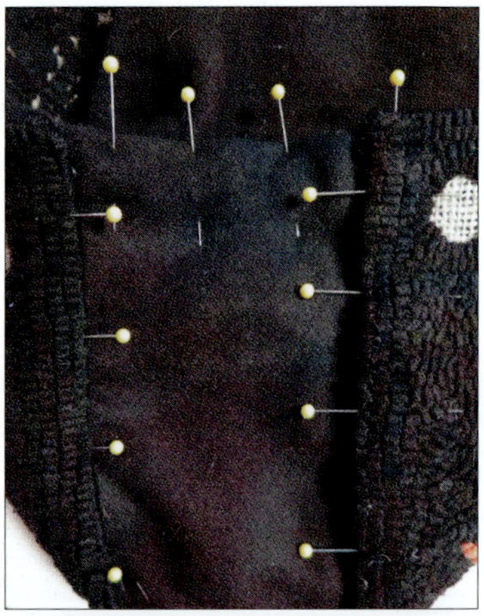

6. Pin the lining and hooked panels together, folding side edges in. Baste the lining in place.
7. Sew the sides using a ladder stitch. Do not sew top edges together.

8. Add the magnet. This magnet can be purchased at a craft store.

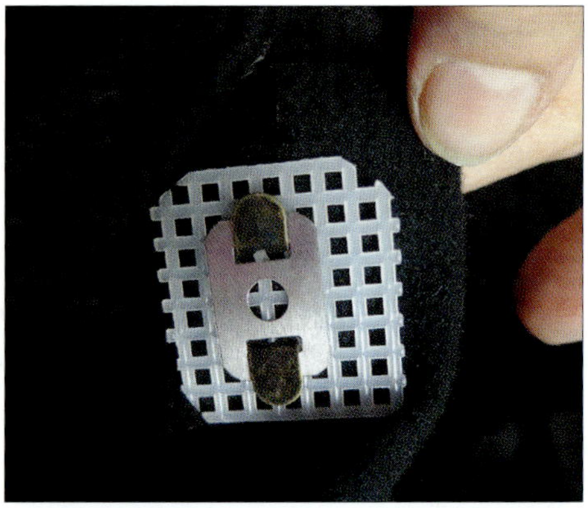

- Fit the lining to top edge and pin.
- Remove the pins from the center section; measure 1" down at the center front and center back panel.
- Cut two small slits in the lining and reinforcing material.
- Push the magnet through the lining and attach the magnet to the lining using plastic needlepoint canvas on the back to reinforce it.

9. Sew around top of bag. Attach the grommets to the hooked portion of your bag. Then fold the sides of the bag on the crease toward the inside, making sure the four holes line up. Mark the side panel for two more grommets, one on each side of the fold. Make sure the four holes line up perfectly. Attach two grommets through the side panel. No extra reinforcing is necessary for the side panel grommets.
For instructions on inserting grommets, see page 58.

10. This is what the bag will look like when all grommets are attached. Thread the handle through the grommets and sew the ends together. Make sure the seam is hidden at side of the bag.

See patterns on pages 106–107.

KARMA TREE CARPETBAG

Designed, hooked, and constructed by Cindy Irwin

DIMENSIONS
11" x 14" x 6"

WE ALL REMEMBER THE MOVIE "MARY POPPINS" FROM OUR CHILDHOOD. REMEMBER HER MARVELOUS CARPETBAG? To make one as big as Mary's is not practical—it would be too heavy, even if the only contents were a credit card and a tissue. I've designed a smaller, lighter version.

Carpetbags differ from other bags because they have internal frames. In the past, I used a hinged frame, but I had problems with them breaking. I now use a barrel frame; it is much sturdier.

Preparation

Drawing the pattern

This carpetbag is constructed from three pieces: a front, a back, and a side/bottom panel. You will have to size the pattern according to the frame size you are using.

- For the 8½" internal frame, the top of the pattern has to be 8 ½"; the side/bottom strip will be 28½" x 5"
- For the 12" internal frame, the top of the pattern has to be 12"; the side/bottom strip will be 39½" x 5"

Transfer the pattern

1. You can use a light table or Crack Stop to transfer the pattern to the backing. Crack Stop is a material used by plasterers. It has a grid and is sticky on one side so it will not move on the backing while you are tracing the pattern. It can be purchased in rolls at builders' supply stores or online.
2. Enlarge the pattern to exactly fit the internal frame that you are using. If you are using an 8½" internal frame, the top edge of your carpetbag has to be exactly 8½" wide. If you are using a 12" internal frame, the top edge has to be exactly 12" wide.
3. Draw a straight line on the pattern by holding a pencil at an angle and running the point of the pencil in the trough of the linen. Place the edge of the pattern on the pencil line.

MATERIALS

Wool
- 1½-2 yds. background wool
- one dyed color strip, 16" x 2 yd.

Barrel frame: available in two sizes: 8½" and 12". For this bag, I used the 8½" frame.

Feet

Needlepoint plastic

Handles

Magnetic closure strap

Lining fabric
- for 8½" frame: 1 yd.
- for 12" frame: 1¼ yd.

Waxed thread

Attaching gemstones

If you want to add gemstones to your carpetbag, add them now.

See the instructions for adding gemstones on pages 54–55.

Dyeing for your carpetbag—try something different!

This is a method of dyeing that I learned from Pris Buttler. I call it color plan dyeing. I often use a strip of this wool as my color plan for a rug. It is an analogous color plan with a complement. You will use ⅓ of this wool for your carpetbag.

1. This will work with any brand of dyes.
2. Measure a 2–yard piece of wool. Divide the wool into thirds so that you have three 2–yard strips, each 19" wide. Soak one strip in preparation for dyeing. Pleat or accordion-fold the strip of wool into a 12" x 15" pan.
3. Pick five analogous colors. "Analogous" means that the colors are beside each other on the color wheel. For this piece, I used colors ranging from blue to yellow. Now find the middle of your chosen colors (in this case, the center color is green). Then, referring to your color wheel, go straight across the wheel to find the complement of green, which is red. These six colors will be your color plan.
4. Now to dye the wool:
    - Use ¼ tsp. of each color, dissolved in 1cup boiling water (CBW) with ¼ tsp. of citric acid.
    - Pour the colors onto the wool, working it in as you go. Make each color overlap its neighbors just a little.
    - Cover the pan with foil and bake at 250° for one hour.
    - Let the wool cool.
    - When cool, rinse and dry the wool.
    - You will be cutting this strip the "wrong" way, in 2–yard strips cutting across all the colors. As long as you use good quality wool, you won't have any problems cutting perpendicular to the selvage.

5. This wool is blue green through red. The complement is yellow. When cut into strips for hooking, each strip will include the entire range of colors.

Hooking

1. A #4 cut seems to work best for hooking this motif. You can use a #5 or #6 cut for the background. Adjust your hooking before you add three-row edge.
2. First, hook the two pieces that will become the front of the bag and the back. Remember, your

pattern will grow as you hook. Note: You will have to adjust your hooking so that the top remains 8 ½" for the small bag and 12" for the large bag. When you are finished hooking the front panels, make sure they are the same size.

3. Now measure the outside edge of the front and back pieces. That measurement will be the length of your side/bottom panel. You will have to adjust your hooking so that the length of the side/bottom strip will fit the front panel. The side/bottom panel should be hooked vertically, except for the top inch. It is best to hook the top edge of the side/bottom panel horizontally so that you can add or subtract rows if needed.

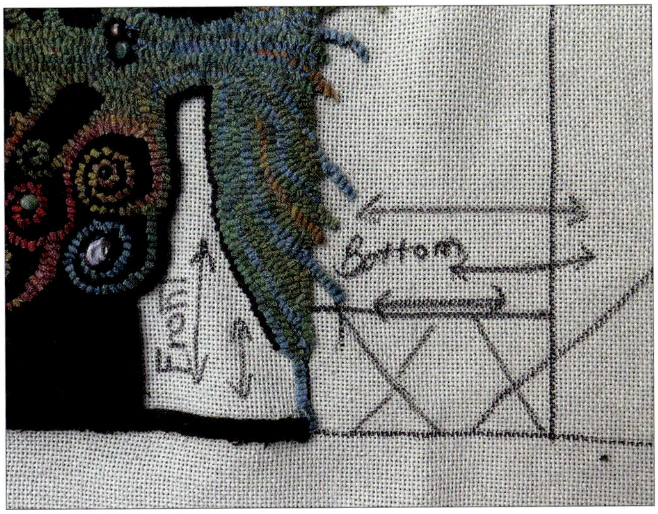

4. When hooking where the bag will fold or bend, it helps to hook in the same direction that the bag will bend. It also helps to pack the wool a little. This will keep the background linen from showing through the hooking.

5. Hook two or three rows around the edges of the carpetbag. The rows should be parallel to the edge of the bag. Hook each row evenly, and pack the wool. This will make it easier to sew the seams together.

6. When hooking around corners, follow the line of your pattern, going down a row of backing as needed to maintain the shape.

7. In the next row, hook in the same loop hole right before going down a row. This will push that loop down and even push out the curve.
8. Measure around sides and bottom of your panels. Adjust the length of side/bottom pattern.

9. When hooking side/bottom panel, hook several rows across top edges. This will allow you to adjust the top of the panel as you put it together.
10. When you are finished hooking, turn the piece over and look for "holidays," those spots where the linen shows, where you skipped hooking. Fill those spots; it will be much easier to hook gaps in your hooking now rather than after the bag is sewn together.
11. Now look at places where the bag will bend (around edges). If it is possible, add another row of hooking.
12. Check the top again. The top of your panels should be exactly 8½" (for an 8½" internal frame), or 12" (for a 12" internal frame).
13. Block thoroughly. If you use gemstones, block carefully on the back side of your hooking

Lining

Make the lining now, using the finished bag pieces as the pattern for the lining. If you use the pattern for the lining, it might be too small. Remember: your hooking grows. For the lining, you will need 1 yd. of fabric, more if you want to add interior pockets.

Construction

1. Serge or zigzag 2" from the side and bottom, and 3" from the top edge of the front and back sections. Serge or zigzag 2" along the long sides of the sides of the bottom panel; serge or zigzag 3" along the two short 5" edges.
2. Sew side seams using the ladder stitch. See the instructions for the ladder stitch on page 49.

3. After sewing side seams, there might be some places you have to go back and hook some more. Make sure you don't hook in the seam opening. Hook through the fold or the overlap seam.

Add feet

For 8½" bag, measure a 4½" x 8½" piece of plastic needlepoint canvas. For 12" bag, measure a 4½" x 12" piece of needlepoint canvas. For installation instructions, see page 56.

Construct the frame channel

You will need:

- For the small 8½" frame: a piece of background wool that is 14" x 4"
- For the large 12" frame: a piece of background wool that is 18" x 4"
- Sew a ½" hem on the two 5" ends. Fold the wrong sides together to make a ¾" pocket for the frame. You now have a piece that is 13" x 2" for an 8" frame, or 17" x 2" for a 12" frame.

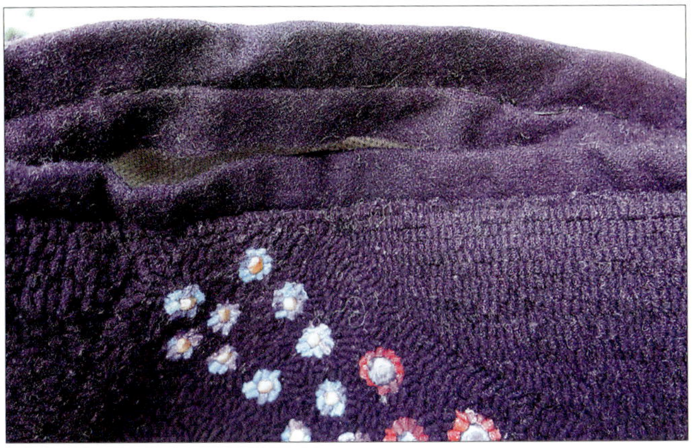

1. Sew the frame channel onto the top of your hooked pieces. You can do this by hand or by machine, using a zipper foot. Press the seams.

2. Go back and hook any spaces where the backing shows.

Attach closure and handles

1. You can buy handles and straps at a craft store, quilt store, or online. Make sure that they have prepunched holes.

2. Mark where you want the handles and center strap. The center strap is necessary; it goes over the top of the bag to hold the sides together. The strap should be around 5½" long.

3. Sew the strap on with heavy thread; upholstery or craft-weight thread will look best.

4. Tack a piece of reinforcing material on the back side of the inside of the bag where you will attach the handles.

5. Now sew handles onto your bag, through this reinforcing material. You can use the plastic reinforcement material that you used for the bottom of the bag, or any heavy fabric. A heavy fabric will be easier to sew through. Artist canvas is the perfect weight; Sunbrella brand fabric is about the same weight.

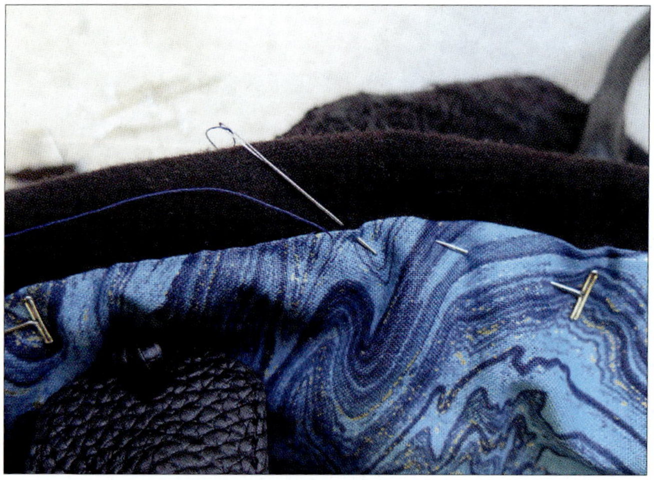

6. Insert the lining into the hooked bag, wrong sides together. Attach the lining to the hooked bag by sewing around the top. Press.

Add the internal frame

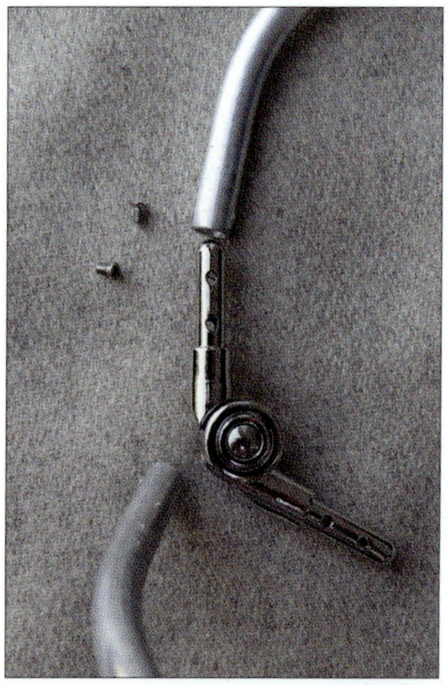

1. Remove the two screws from the hinges on each end of the frame. Place the screws in a safe place so they do not get lost.

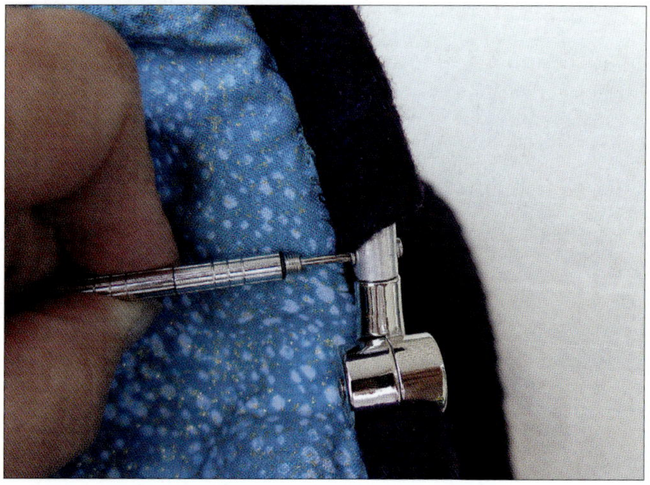

2. Ease the frame through the wool channel, then reattach hinge.

See pattern on page 108.

FLORAL DUFFLE CARPETBAG

Designed, hooked, and constructed by Susan Clarke

CARPET BAGS COME IN A VARIETY OF STYLES. This bag is fashioned after the simple duffle bag available for sale at many stores, and at 30" long, it is about the same size. As you might guess, this bag was originally destined to be a rug; I hooked it in a workshop with Canadian teacher Ingrid Hieronomus. While I loved her *Flower Garden* design and the way she taught her technique of wide-cut shading with her specially dyed spot dyes, I just didn't have a place in my home for this rug.

I had tried my hand before at making a carpetbag and I enjoyed the process, so I decided to "repurpose" this great rug into a carpetbag. It was a good idea, as now I use it all the time. It is great as a project bag for my hooking, especially when I need to carry all my wools and project. It is also terrific as a suitcase—I don't ever worry that someone might pick it up by accident because it looks like every other suitcase!

MATERIALS

Main body piece—Options:

Option A: Purchased rug hooking pattern. Illustrations show *Flower Garden* (available from Ragg Tyme Studio), already hooked. This hooked rug will be turned into the duffle bag.

Option B: 1¼ yd. linen (or other backing) and materials for hooking the body of the bag (if doing your own design)

Contrasting wool or leather pieces, to fit pattern

Lining: 1½ yard (54" or more wide) colorful indoor/outdoor fabric

Long rolled leather handles: 1 set. Illustrations show handles purchased from Fish Eye Sisters

Heavy duty or upholstery thread

Specialty sewing machine needles, for sewing leather

Strong T-pins

Metal 2-way heavy duty zipper

Fabric adhesive spray (optional)

For best results, confirm the measurements of the rug you choose to use or the pattern you purchase. The width should be between 30" to 38" (for a 9½" to 12" diameter end), and the length should be between 24" to 30". Check that the orientation of the design is correct! It is important that you know in the instructions to follow, that the width is the longer measurement because it will wrap around the ends of the duffle.

Preparation

The duffle bag was simple to make. I had to do some math to figure out the diameter of the ends, and I had to learn how to sew with leather. I had trouble getting a perfect match between the leather I used for the ends and purchased leather handles, so I ended up making my own handles. Not as difficult as you would think, but I had to purchase a tool that punched holes, and then hand sew the leather over cording and buy the hardware. I was on a roll with the handles, so I decided to make a long shoulder strap and attach it to the ends. This has come in handy when I am carrying projects to workshops because it leaves my hands free for my hooking frame.

For this project, rug hooking skills are essential; sewing skills not so much. But you do need a basic knowledge of sewing. If you are not a competent seamstress, a friend who is should be able to help you finish your bag.

I recommend buying your handles first. They will help you to decide on your color palette. The rug design can be a pattern you purchase or one you design yourself. For a really custom piece, choose your lining fabric first, and then base your hooking design on that. This will make it a really stunning, sophisticated piece. Or, if you are like me, look around for a rug you aren't using and repurpose it!

As You Plan

Here are a few tips to keep in mind for a dynamite carpetbag.

- Be sure the design on the hooking is oriented correctly for your bag.
- The impact of this bag is all about the colors and the customized elements.
- When choosing a hooked design or creating your own design, keep it simple and colorful.
- I recommend buying the lining first, and developing your hooking design based on the lining. It is much easier than finding the perfect lining for an already hooked piece, and this adds to the custom look of the completed piece.

Hooking

In these instructions, I use the rug illustrated here. However, choose a size that best meets your needs and follow these instructions to pull it all together.

Option A: Using a "pre-made" hooked rug

For this project, I used my previously hooked rug *Flower Garden* (pattern designed by Ingrid Hieronomus).

1. Remove the whipping from the edge of the rug.
2. Remove the remainder of the finishing you used on your rug. (In my rugs, I usually leave around 1 ½" of backing, cover a cotton cord, and slipstitch it in place before whipping. Undo all of this!)
3. Cut the excess backing away, leaving only about ½" seam allowance around the perimeter of your rug. Serge the edges or zigzag with your sewing machine. If zigzagging, go around the rug several times.
4. Re-press the rug.

Option B: Creating a new hooked piece

1. Purchase a hooking pattern in your desired size, or design your own rug. My rug was approximately 30" x 38".
2. Before you begin, look at duffle bags for sale in stores and choose a size that looks good and works for you. If I were going to do a new bag, I would probably reduce the length to about 24". I would keep the diameter the same (12"); this diameter works out to a circumference of 38" (your rug's width) and would result in a bag 38" wide. In other words, your width is much longer than your length.
3. Hook the design in your color palette.
4. Press the hooked piece and allow to dry flat.
5. Cut the front hooked piece from the backing; leave ½" seam allowance all around. Serge the edges or zigzag with your sewing machine. If zigzagging, go around the piece several times.

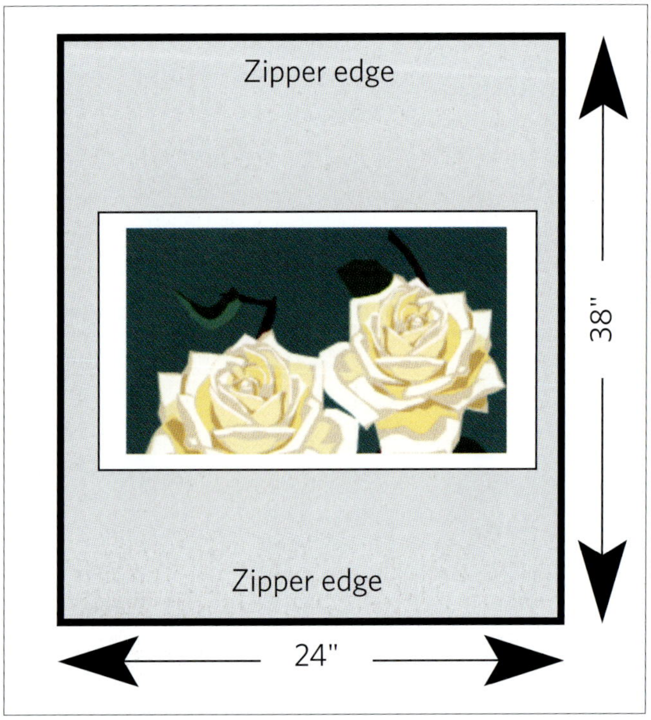

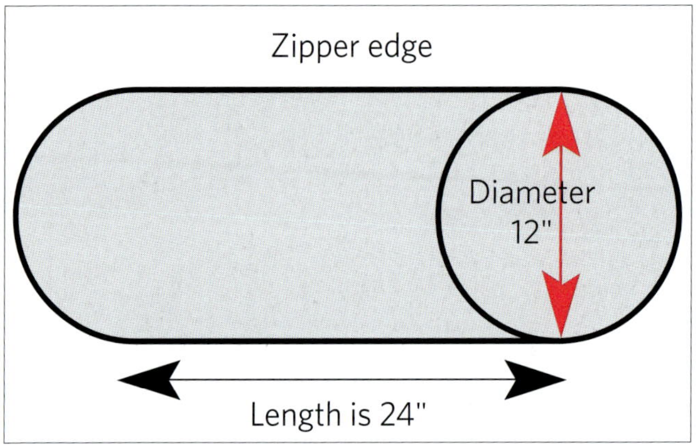

Dimensions and orientation of bag (note the zipper edge is called the length)

Making the carpetbag

(*These instructions work for either option*)

1. Measure the hooked dimensions of the main body piece.
    - The width of the hooked rug will be the circumference of the ends of the finished bag.
    - The length will be the edge where the zipper is sewn.
2. Determine the size of the carpetbag ends. See the box with instructions on how to determine this.
3. On construction paper or brown paper, draw a circle the size of your calculated diameter. Draw a second circle ½" larger, around that first circle. This indicates your seam allowance. Now you have the pattern for your end pieces.
4. Cut two end pieces of fabric or leather, making sure to include the ½" seam allowance. It looks best when the color of the ends matches the background color of your hooked piece. The end pieces should match your handles.

Lining

1. Choose your lining. I purchase indoor/outdoor fabric for the lining of my carpetbags. These fabrics are relatively inexpensive, easy to sew, and they wear extremely well. And best of all, they come in a wonderful variety of colors and patterns.
2. Wash the lining fabric, dry, and press.
3. Lay your pressed rug and the two end pieces on top of the lining fabric. Pin in place (or use fabric adhesive) and cut lining pieces the same size as the hooked and fabric/leather pieces. Serge or zigzag around the edges.

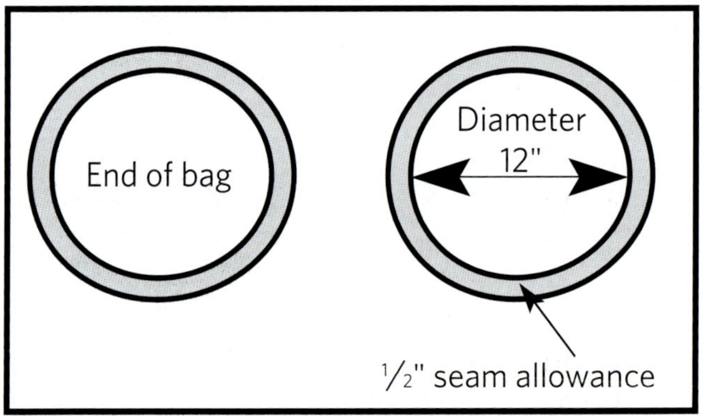

A MATH REVIEW

Remember high school geometry? Now you have an opportunity to put it to practical use!

Let's figure out the size of the carpetbag ends. You will need to do some simple math, or use the handy table below.

Circumference is the measurement of the outside edge of the circle ends. In our case, the circumference of the end circles is the same as the width of the flat rug.

- The formula is: $C = \pi \times d$
- C is circumference; d is diameter; $\pi = 3.14$"
- Here is an example: If a rug width is 38", that means that the end circle circumference will be 38". Divide 38 by 3.14 and you get a diameter of 12". Now you know your end circle will have a diameter of 12".
- If your rug is any other width, you need to do the following calculations: divide the width of your rug by π (3.14). The answer will be the diameter of your end circles.

$$D = \frac{\text{width}}{\pi}$$

I have provided a handy table for you with some possible measurements.

Standard End Diameters	
Rug Width (W)	**End Diameter (D)**
38"	12"
36"	11.5"
34.5"	11"
33"	10.5"
31.5"	10"
30"	9.5"

Assembling the bag

1. **Assemble the bag lining.** I always sew the lining first, as it is easier to catch and correct a mistake here.
   - With right sides together, pin the two long sides of the main body together. Sew together at each end, 1½" from the edge in toward the center. Do not sew the section in between, because this is where your zipper will be sewn in later.

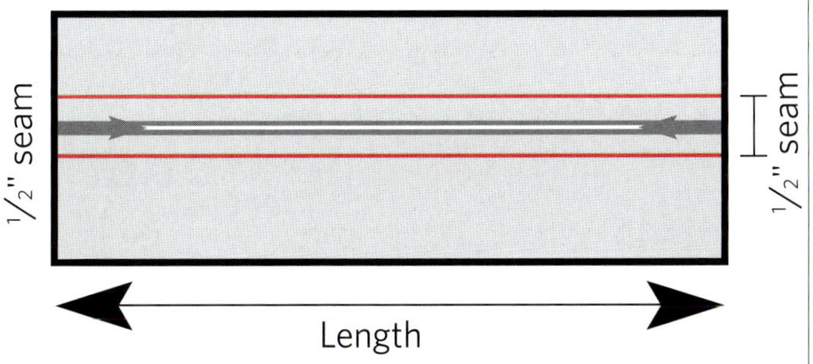

   - Press the seam allowance down, the full length of both length sides. Topstitch ¼" from fold/seam, using a long stitch setting. This will create a nice finished edge for the zipper and also fasten down the two end seams, as you can see in the diagram.
   - With right sides together, pin the width edge of the main body piece around the circumference of one circle end piece. Baste by hand along the ½" seam allowance. Make adjustments as you baste. Repeat on the other end.
   - Using your sewing machine, sew each end piece to the main body piece along the basted seams. Remove the basting. Press the seam allowance toward the main body piece. Topstitch with a long stitch, about ¼" from the seam.
2. **Attach the zipper to the hooked exterior.**
   - Press down the seam allowance along the length of the bag.
   - Separate the two halves of the zipper. Pin one zipper half to one side (sew the upper side of the zipper to the turned over seam allowance), and sew it on using a zipper foot

and long sewing stitch. (Note: You will probably have to release the tension to accommodate the thickness of the rug, turned under seam allowance, and zipper.) Use upholstery thread on the top and use bobbin thread in the bobbin. The zipper should be the same length as the hooked length of the bag, less the length of the end seams. So, in my 30" bag, the zipper teeth should measure about 27" (30" – 3").

- Now zip up the zipper. Line up the ends of the bag length; pin the second zipper half to the second bag length. Sew using a long stitch.

3. **Assemble the carpetbag exterior.**
   - With right sides together, pin the width edge of the hooked main body piece around the circumference of one circle end piece. Baste together by hand, along the ½" seam allowance. Make adjustments as you baste. If using a longer zipper, make sure to "sandwich" it between the hooked main body and the leather end so that it sits properly. Repeat at the other end.
   - Machine stitch each end piece to the main body along the basted seams. Remove the basting. Press the seam allowance toward the main body piece.

Handles and finishing touches

1. Center your purchased handles on each side of the bag, placing the tabs close to the top. I recommend adding a small piece of sturdy fabric (such as the fabric you can purchase for jean repairs) on the back side of your rug to stabilize the area for the handle tab, lined up with the handle tab. This can be lightly basted in place, or you can use fabric adhesive spray instead of basting. Hand stitch the handle tab firmly in place, going through the hooking and the new piece of fabric on the back of the hooking.
2. Insert the lining into the hooked bag with the wrong sides together. Line up the finished open edges of the lining with the underside of the zipper on the interior of the hooked carpet bag. Pin the lining to the bag along the underside of the zipper, leaving the zipper teeth free. Baste the lining to the bag exterior, using a slip stitch. In the future, if you need to wash the interior, you can just clip these stitches to remove the lining for laundering.
3. Add a personalized label to the lining, giving your name and any other information you wish.

BLISS BAG

Designed, hooked, and constructed by Jen Manuell

DIMENSIONS
14" x 14"

IN THE SPRING OF 2002, I WAS EXCITEDLY PLANNING MY FIRST VISIT TO NEW YORK CITY, WHEN I DISCOVERED MY TRIP WOULD COINCIDE WITH THE INAUGURAL HOOKED RUG DAY AT THE AMERICAN FOLK ART MUSEUM. Of course, I found a way to fit *that* into my plans! I immediately started brainstorming to come up with something I could wear to make it obvious I was a rug hooker.

It was my Mum who made the brilliant suggestion I should hook and sew a purse. After a couple of weeks playing with idea—mostly trying to figure out a good way to "bridge the gap" between the end of the hooking and the beginning of the trim—I came up with a solution: start with a long, flat piece of hooking, make it into a tube, and then sew an oval-shaped base on one end to make the bottom of the bag. Like most things, of course, my vision and a satisfactory outcome were far apart, and the process of finishing and actually turning the flat piece of hooking into a purse was a painful version of "two steps forward and one step back," on repeat.

I learned a good deal with that first bag, and yes, it was finished in time and attracted attention. In fact, the response was so amazing I went on to create a few more purses . . . and then a few more . . . and then things snowballed. It was not long before I was asked to teach a workshop and share how to make my bags. Selling patterns quickly followed, and then new designs, new constructions, and more invitations to teach.

The Bliss Bag is the result of years of experimentation with a variety of different construction methods. If you already have basic rug hooking skills and supplies, know how to operate a sewing machine and a needle and a pair of scissors, then you can make the Bliss Bag. It's still true that having a hooked bag on your arm quickly announces you as a rug hooker—or at least the very good friend of one!

Preparation

Choose handles or strap

Select the handles or a strap for your bag pretty early on. Choosing your handles or strap now will allow you to incorporate colors into your hooking that tie in with the color of the handles or strap. It is a million times easier to match your hooking to the handles than to find handles or a strap that match your hooking.

Design your motifs

I've intentionally left the paper pattern blank in hopes you will experiment and create your own design. I suggest you use a pencil and try out your ideas on the paper pattern, and then commit with marker when you are happy with your design. If you like the simple crosses motif, you are welcome to copy it. I just hooked the crosses freestyle, keeping the number of loops consistent (seven on each line with a "crossover" on the back where they intersect).

Make a cardboard template

1. Glue cardboard template A to a piece of medium-weight cardboard using a regular glue stick. Line up the straight edge of the template with a straight edge of the cardboard.
2. Cut away the excess paper and cardboard on the inside of the heavy black line.
3. Cut away the excess paper on the inside of the heavy black line of template B.
4. Glue template B to the back side of the same piece of cardboard (so the template is double-sided), making sure the straight edge of the template is lined up with the straight edge of the cardboard.

MATERIALS

Handles or a strap: I prefer the simplicity, beauty, and high quality of My Leather long rolled handles (available in our online store), but of course, the possibilities for handles or a strap for this bag are endless. Use your imagination and repurpose an old belt, handles from an old purse, pieces of Ultrasuede or leather, or design and make your own handles or strap with coordinating fabric.

Rug warp: 36" long x 20" across. This size allows ample room for the two halves of the bag plus 3" to 3½" of rug warp at the outside edges in all directions. Use a larger piece if more free border is desired. Use rug warp rather than linen to provide shape and structure to your finished bag. Press your rug warp to be sure it is nice and flat before transferring the pattern.

Trim: Wool flannel trim fabric, 1"–1¼" wide by 26" long. Use good quality wool, tightly woven and fulled, with very little nap, as it will be less likely to "pill." Choose a color to coordinate with your hooking. If you prefer, tear a strip 1½" wide and then trim it to 1¼" with a rotary cutter and ruler after fusing it with the interfacing.

Fusible knit interfacing: 1"–1¼"wide by about 26" long. I use this bit of interfacing to add strength and durability to the wool trim fabric. This interfacing adheres the best and does not shift from handling. You will also need a couple of scraps about 1½" square for the optional magnetic closure. Adjust the width of the interfacing to 1½" if you plan to fuse it to the trim fabric, and then trim them both together to 1¼" afterward.

Lining fabric: ½ yd. I like 100% cotton batiks (available at quilting stores), mostly because they are beautiful, but also because there is no real right or wrong side, they are fairly durable, batiks complement hand-dyed wools used in hooking, and a little bit of batik fabric adds a little something extra to the finished product. Use the same fabric for the lining and the optional pocket, or try two different batiks to add interest to the inside of the bag. I wait and choose batiks after the hooking is completed.

Coordinating pocket fabric: ⅓ yd.

Magnetic closure, optional

Scissors for cutting paper

Medium cardboard: Something like a cereal box, to glue the paper template to.

Glue stick

Scotch/masking/washi tape

Black permanent marker

Ruler or measuring tape

Pencil

Sharpie Rub-a-Dub Fabric Marker

Thread for machine & hand sewing: suitable thread to coordinate with your lining fabric.

Sewing machine

Scissors for cutting fabric

Tapestry needle: Choose one with a blunt end instead of a point, but not as large as a bodkin.

Upholstery (or extra strong) thread: Choose any color for sewing the bag together. We usually use dark brown or black to coordinate with our favorite My Leather handles.

Large safety pins, about 15

18-gauge syringe needle

Pins

Marking wheel and papers or a colored marking pencil

Needle and optional thimble for hand sewing

Transfer the outline and pattern to rug warp

1. Fold one short edge of the rug warp in half and mark the center with a pencil (the mark should be about 10" from each side).
2. Place the rug warp flat on a firm table top.
3. Hold the pencil at a low angle on the center mark, and then firmly run the pencil along the rug warp to make a centerline down the length of the rug warp, perfectly straight with the weave of the rug warp.
4. Hold the pencil at an angle on the line approximately 9" from the short end, and then run the pencil along the rug warp across the width (approx. 20").
5. Repeat step 4 to draw a perpendicular pencil line 9" in from the other end.
6. Place the cardboard template you just made onto the rug warp. Line up the straight edge of the template with the center pencil line and the dotted line on the template with a perpendicular pencil line. Stretch and nudge the rug warp until both pencil lines on the rug warp are perfectly aligned with the template. Sometimes rug warp gets skewed from being wound on the bolt, and I don't want this to distort the shape of your finished bag.
7. Hold the template firmly in place, and then carefully trace around the outside curved edges and darts (but not along the straight center line) of the template with a Sharpie Rub-A-Dub to draw half of one side of the bag.
8. Flip the template over and repeat steps 6 and 7 to finish drawing the first side of the bag.
9. Turn the rug warp 180° and repeat steps 6 through 8 to draw the second side of the bag.
10. Tape the paper pattern (with your motifs drawn on) to a bright window at eye level (or use a light box). Align and match up the cardboard template outline you just drew on the rug warp with the outline of the paper pattern beneath. You can move the rug warp and hold it in place with your hand, rather than trying to tape it exactly in place. (The tape just helps to support some of the weight.)
11. Transfer your motifs onto the rug warp with a Sharpie Rub-A-Dub. Check alignment as you go.
12. Repeat steps 10 and 11 to transfer your motifs to the rug warp for the other side of the bag.

Hooking

Read through this section before you get started on your hooking. A few moments spent now may help to avoid frustration later.

Experiment

Don't be afraid to try something new! A purse is a small project (relative to most other hooking adventures) and is a great opportunity to let yourself go and try new ideas without investing a lot of time or money in supplies. It only takes a few evenings to hook each side. Once you've pulled your last loop, you can always rehook any parts that don't appeal to you. Try working with different cuts, colors, textures, and/or alternative fibers.

Use your favorite cuts of wool. I used #8-cut wool strips for our version, but this rug hooking project is adaptable to other cuts. I often add bits of sari ribbon, selvedges, and chunky yarns, plus my own hand-dyed slub wool, to add texture, sheen, and interest.

Color Planning Tips

Purses are great projects for using up leftovers—the more variety, the better! I easily use more than 50 different wools in a hooked bag. Keep in mind that many subtleties lost on a rug will be noticed on a purse, since a purse is almost always viewed up close.

Use a number of short strips in the same color family to achieve interesting motifs and generate movement. I use small amounts of many wools, rather than larger amounts of just a few wools—little bits of leftovers from previous projects are great for this. Add a variety of yarns and ribbons: if a yarn is thin, combine several strands of the same yarn or a couple of different yarns together and hook them as one. Work these in alongside wool strips to add interest and depth. Yarn is also great for filling in small or irregular areas. Too much texture can get caught on jewelry, so be careful to keep textured loops flush with the rest of your hooking.

Don't labor over the color planning. A purse is a very personal accessory. It should work with your personality and wardrobe, not match your sofa and a painting above the bookcase! If you can shop for your own clothes, you can choose colors for your purse—just look in your closet for inspiration!

Remember to combine a variety of textures and values for a background with movement and interest. I use 12 to 14 or more different wools in the background of a purse, the majority of which are the same basic value, with a couple of pieces slightly darker and a few a little bit lighter. Make sure the outliers are well dispersed.

Hooking

While using rug warp, make sure your backing is as tight as possible on your frame (to open up the holes). Try using a larger hook than you normally use.

I hook bags from one side to the other, filling in background as I hook each motif, for several reasons. This helps retain its size and shape. Not only does this appeal to my laziness gene (I don't have to move the pattern around on my frame as much), it gives me a more realistic idea of what the finished product will be like earlier in the process, while also providing a soft place to rest my hooking hand. Plus, there is no boring background left at the end.

Don't over-pack your loops. There is a fine line between too much and too little packing when you're hooking a purse. Without a certain amount of packing, your backing might be visible after construction. But too much packing can lead to distortion, especially within the shapes of motifs. If there is too much space left between the rows (particularly in the 1" to 1 ½" areas along the sides and bottoms that will later curve once the bag is assembled), it may inadvertently cause a natural fold once the bag is assembled, creating a gap and even showing the backing underneath. If this happens, pull up several loops of yarn or narrow wool strips in the valley after your purse is sewn together—it's a little awkward since it's not on a frame, but you can do it!

Hook right up to the drawn lines on the outside edges of each piece. When hooking along the top edge, hook just inside the line and use good quality wool since this is one of the areas of your purse that will receive the most wear and tear. On the sides and bottom (where you will later be joining the two halves of the bag together), don't hook along the outside lines, since it can draw attention to the seam and make it more obvious. Instead, break up the line by using short pieces of wool and making random detours into the adjoining background.

Leave tails uncut along the outside edge and around the darts (about ⅛" to ¼" higher than your hooked loops). It is easy to trim these tails too short, which will make your seam more noticeable when assembled. Instead, wait to trim these tails when the bag is sewn together.

When hooking overlapping motifs that span both sides of the purse, use pieces of the same wool strip. This trick will camouflage your seams. Your hooking will appear to carry across the seam, rather than conspicuously all ending at the seam.

Only one side of your purse will ever be seen at a time, so don't worry about running out of any particular wool because I promise that no one will notice!

Finishing

Once the hooking is completed, don't procrastinate! Read these simple finishing instructions carefully and follow my suggestions. Remember: any hooked bag assembly requires more patience than skill. You will be surprised how easy it is to turn your beautiful hooked piece into a high-quality handmade one-of-a-kind bag!

1. Press your finished hooked piece. I use heavy steam, a wet cloth, and an iron. Lay flat to cool and dry. Vacuum the piece thoroughly at this stage to remove as much lint as possible.
2. Draw a curved line carefully with a marker on the backside of each hooked piece: first, at ½" away from the last row of hooking around the sides and bottom, and then ¾" away from the hooking along the top edges. Ignore the darts, just continue drawing your line past them (don't indent). Take your time. It is important to keep the distance between the lines and your hooking as even as possible, especially along the top edge.

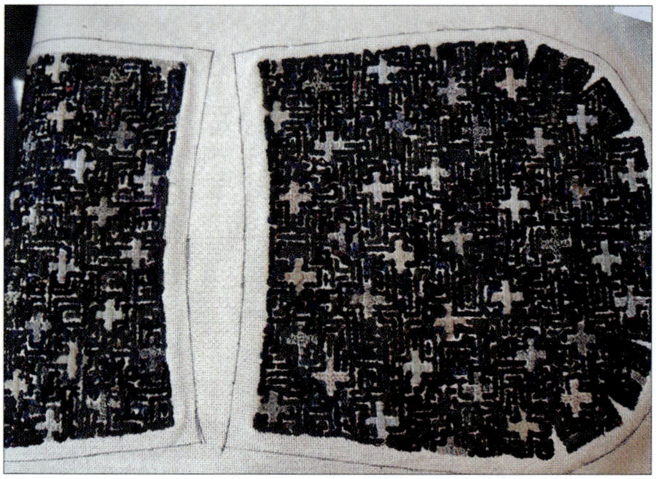

There are two methods to draw these lines:

- Use a skinny, clear quilting ruler and hold it parallel to and lined up ½" from the edge, and then rotate it with the curve and draw a smooth line along the edge of the ruler as you go.
- Use a regular ruler and hold it perpendicular to the edge. Run it along the edge and make dots on the rug warp every couple of inches, then draw a smooth line to join the dots.

3. Machine stitch along all the curved lines just inside the drawn line, using a "stretch" zigzag stitch. Then repeat and go around a second time for good measure.
    - The "stretch" zigzag stitch makes multiple stitches from side-to-side as it is formed. This stretch zigzag stitch catches more individual threads, which provides a stable edge with little potential for fraying. It holds everything together much better than even a serged edge. The symbol for stretch zigzag is a dotted or dashed zigzag line.
    - Use the edge of your hooking as a guide for the presser foot. Sewing with the loops face down is easier—the loops don't get caught up on the presser foot.
    - Use a contrasting thread to make it easy to see the stitches for trimming in the next step.

4. Trim hooked pieces along the drawn line, right to the edge of the zigzag stitching.
5. Prepare a tapestry needle with upholstery thread. Remove excess twist and tie the ends together with a double or granny knot to create a doubled thread.

6. Hold one hooked half of the bag at a dart, with the right side of your hooking facing up. Pinch the dart together, and then tuck and fold the rug warp into the seam. If you are right handed, hold your work so the point of the dart is on your left and the rug warp seam allowance is on your right. Reverse if you are left handed. You may find it helps to extend the dart lines through the rug warp seam with a black marker.
7. Sew the dart closed with ladder stitch (in the same manner you would use to sew the seams of a sweater together), starting at the zigzag edge. Be sure to catch the threads of rug warp between the hooked loops and/or as close to the hooked loops as possible, but be careful not to catch any wool or wrap around any loops with your upholstery thread. Catch only the threads of the rug warp in your stitches. Take your time. Make sure you have a good light and that each dart is "invisible" when finished. This will contribute to the overall appearance of your finished bag. Sewing the darts and side seams is the most tedious part. Take a break and split this up into a couple of sessions.

JEN'S LADDER STITCH INSTRUCTIONS

Upholstery thread glides easily through rug warp.

1. Weave your needle through a few threads of the rug warp, and then pull up your needle in the same hole as the first loop of hooking at the outside edge of one side of the dart. Pass your needle under the thread of rug warp in line and immediately across on the other side of the dart, and then continue to weave your needle and upholstery thread from top to bottom *catching the threads of rug warp between the hooked loops on both sides* to close the dart (see photos). Be sure for every stitch you make to always point your needle in the direction you need to go to close the dart. Gently pull out the slack in your upholstery thread with each stitch, but do not pull it tight. Wait and pull it tight every 1" to 1½" or so.
2. To pull tight, pinch the outer seam allowance, and then pull the thread firmly in a straight line in the opposite direction (until the thread is taut and the dart closes completely). Be sure to wait to pull tight only after every 1" to 1½" of sewing. Waiting makes it easier to see where to take the next stitch, but waiting too long (more than 1½") will make it difficult to pull out all of the slack. If you don't have a lot of hand strength, pull tight more often (try every ¾" to 1" instead).

8. To complete the dart, bring the needle through to the back (wrong side) at the point of the dart, and then secure the end of the thread. Check the front side and trim any wool tails flush with your hooked loops. You may need to lengthen or shorten a loop or two by tugging on adjacent loops and/or tails.
9. Sew the seam allowance of the dart closed. Bring the needle back up in the same spot at the outside edge of the bag (where you began to sew the dart closed). Sew with ladder stitch out to the edge of the seam allowance and tie off and trim the end of the thread.
10. Repeat steps 5 through 9 for the other 11 darts. If small gaps appear between your hooked loops after sewing the darts, hide them by placing a few delicate and hidden "secret stitches" to hold the loops together.
11. Baste the top edge of one half of the bag with a tapestry needle and upholstery thread. Fold

the rug warp seam allowance in half toward the wrong side (the inside). Start sewing 1" in from the side edge of the hooking (that is, about 1½" from the outside edge). Whip stitch the folded seam allowance in place with upholstery thread and stitches placed about ¼" apart. Take care to sew through both layers of rug warp and to secure your stitches by making them as tall as the zigzag stitching. Stop sewing 1" from where the hooking ends (again, about 1½" from the outside edge). Leave long tails of upholstery thread (so you may use them to re-thread the needle and baste the rest of the folded edge once the two halves of the bag are joined together). Double thread your needle—that is, thread the eye twice in the same direction. This can act as a temporary "lock" of sorts and make it less likely the thread will pull through the needle and require re-threading. Take care not to catch any hooked loops in your stitches.

12. Repeat step 11 with the other side of the bag.
13. Match and align the two sides of the bag with the hooked loops facing out.
14. Start at one top corner and tuck the rug warp edges into the seam; use a large safety pin to hold the two pieces aligned and together at the top corner (pinning right through the hooked loops).
15. Continue to tuck and safety pin at each pair of aligned darts and the other top corner of the bag.
16. Match and safety pin each overlapping stem or other motif, if any, along the bottom and/or sides of the bag.
17. Match and safety pin the remainder of the bag every 2" or so to hold the two pieces aligned along the sides and bottom of the bag. (Ignore the top edge for now.)

18. Hand stitch the side seam with a tapestry needle and upholstery thread, using the same methods we showed you to sew the darts closed in steps 7 through 9.
    - For a seamless appearance, look ahead to the next pin to be sure the two sides stay aligned. One side may have more loops than the other; if so, adjust your stitches to compensate. A careful but thorough steaming of the bag with an iron and shots of steam will smooth out distortions and relax the seam.
    - Take the time to read through steps 7 through 9 carefully to refresh your memory. Be sure to remove the excess twist from your thread and to go back and sew the seam allowance closed at the end.
19. Fold and baste the two short sections of seam allowance along the top edge that we ignored earlier so that the top edge of the bag has a continuous folded edge. Fold the rug warp seam allowance to the inside, and then baste in place with whip stitch. Trim away a small amount of excess to reduce bulk, but take care not to compromise stability.
20. Prepare a standard sewing needle with thread to match your trim fabric.
21. Preparing the trim:
    - Place the trim fabric right side facing down on an ironing surface, then place the fusible knit interfacing on top with the glue dots face down and the smooth side face up. Use scissors to trim the interfacing even with the outside edges of the wool flannel before fusing.
    - Fuse with a warm iron, following product instructions. Use a straight down motion, hold for about three seconds, lift the iron up and off, and then over and straight down again. Use a setting between wool and cotton with no steam.
    - Place an old pillowcase or large scrap of fabric on your ironing surface to protect it from bits of interfacing adhesive.
22. You may prefer to finish the top edge of your bag by whipping with yarn. We have used both methods and find the fabric trim tends to wear better—plus it's a lot faster!

Sewing My Leather Handles

Use a tapestry needle and upholstery thread, doubled, and sew on top of the hooking and firmly right through the backing. I use an 18-gauge syringe needle to help guide the needle through from the back to the front of the hooking. Simply press the syringe needle through the hole in the leather, then place the tip of your needle into the end of the syringe needle from the back side of your hooking, and push both back through to the front side.

23. Attach the trim fabric. Place a short edge of the trim fabric near a side seam of the bag and butt a long edge of the trim fabric up to the top row of hooked loops, with right side facing up and the opening of the bag facing you. Hand stitch the trim fabric in place, assuring that there is no backing visible between the hooking and the trim fabric. Use small "invisible" stitches between the hooked loops and catch a small amount of trim in each stitch. Continue until the circuit is complete. Cut off the excess trim fabric so that the two ends overlap by ¼", and then sew through both layers to secure the end. Nudge up and hold your trim fabric where you want it to be before you pull your thread tight.
24. Fold the trim fabric firmly over the folded seam allowance, and stitch in place on the inside of the bag. Place stitches ¼" to ⅜" apart and make sure to sew right through the rug warp backing, not just the backs of your hooked loops.

25. Attach the handles or strap according to product instructions. Helpful hints are in the box on page 90.

26. Press the lining fabric, and then place it flat on a firm table top. Fold the fabric to double it (enough to cut two of the lining pattern from the fabric at the same time). Lay the lining pattern on top and pin securely in place.
27. Cut around the lining pattern through both layers of the lining fabric to cut the two halves of the lining.
28. Mark the darts on the wrong sides of both halves of the lining. Use a marking wheel and contrasting marking papers to draw the lines, or use a colored pencil. You can include more complicated features in your bag lining construction, like zippers or extra pockets. Modify the lining to suit your needs.
29. Pin each dart together, and then machine stitch all 12 darts closed.
30. Press the pocket fabric, and then repeat steps 27 and 28 with the pocket pattern to cut the two layers of fabric for the pocket.
31. Assemble the two halves of the pocket with right sides together, and then pin along the outside edges. Note: there is a 6" section at the bottom which will not be sewn.
32. Machine stitch with a ¼" seam allowance along the outside edge and around the top, from one bottom corner to the other (leaving about 6" unsewn). Clip the top corners and seam allowance curves, taking care to cut close to, but not through, the sewing.

33. Turn the pocket pieces right side out and press the seam, folding the seam allowance into the middle and maintaining the curved shape.
34. Topstitch along the seam of the top curved edge to add stability and detail to the top edge of the pocket piece. Press.
35. Place the pocket right side up in the center of one half of the lining. Pin in place.
36. Machine stitch the outside curved edge of the pocket to the lining. Reinforce the beginning and end of your stitching at the top edge of the pocket, as these are significant stress points in the finished bag.
37. Pin the two halves of lining together, right sides together.
38. Machine stitch around the sides and bottom (not the top) of the lining with a ½" seam allowance.
39. Fold back a ½" seam around the top of the lining and press to hold the fold; this will provide a smooth edge when the lining is hand sewn into the bag.
40. Attach the magnetic closure according to product instructions.
41. Attach the lining. Place the lining inside the bag, wrong sides together. Line up the side seams of the lining and the hooked bag, and pin in place. Leave an even strip (about ¼") of trim fabric visible between the top edge and the lining fabric. Find the center of each half of the lining and each half of the bag and pin those together, then ease and pin the rest of the lining within each quadrant.
42. Hand stitch the lining to the trim fabric with coordinating thread and small "invisible" stitches.
43. Hand stitch about six tiny stitches around each half of the magnetic closure to secure it in place. Stitch right through the rug warp, as this area will be a stress point in the finished bag.
44. Tack the lining to the bag in a couple of places along the side seams and along the center seam of the pocket, if desired.

See patterns on pages 109–110.

PATTERNS

USE THESE PATTERNS TO MAKE YOUR OWN HOOKED BAG. Dimensions are provided so that you can enlarge the patterns and reproduce the bags as they are shown in each chapter. These patterns are for personal use only.

Hooker's Drawstring Bag

Size to fit your bag

Bohemian Banded Bag

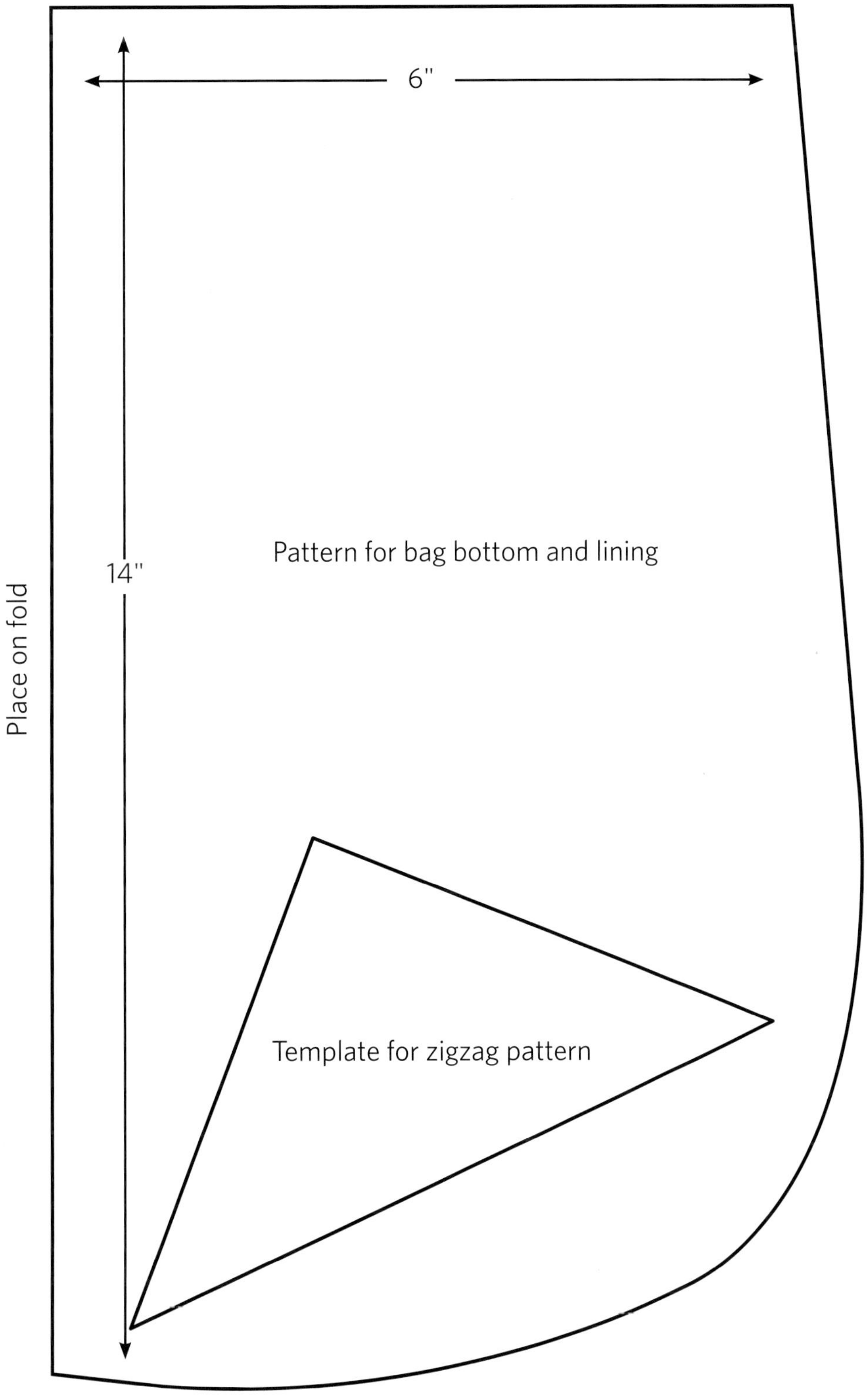

"Flower Power" Handbag

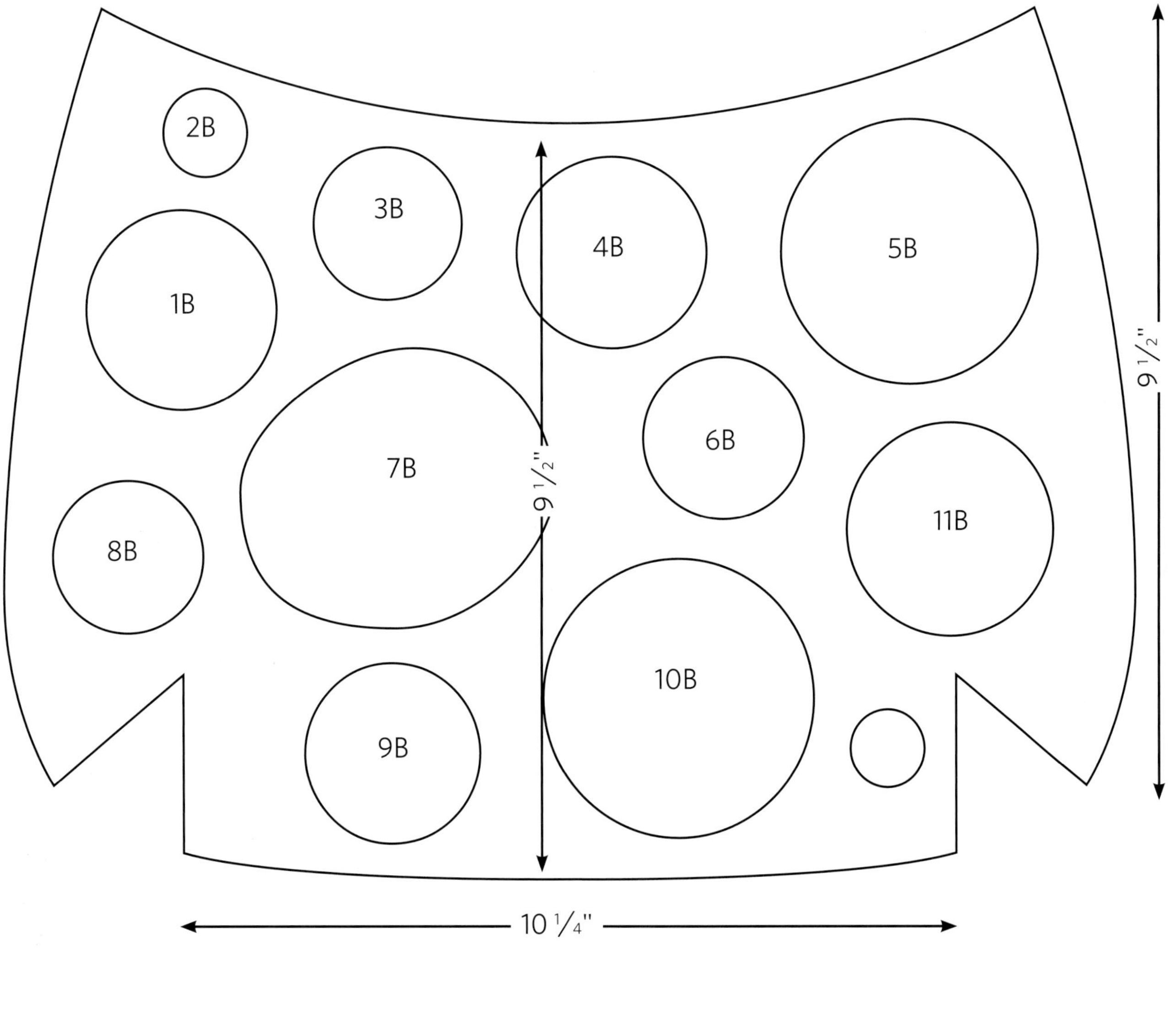

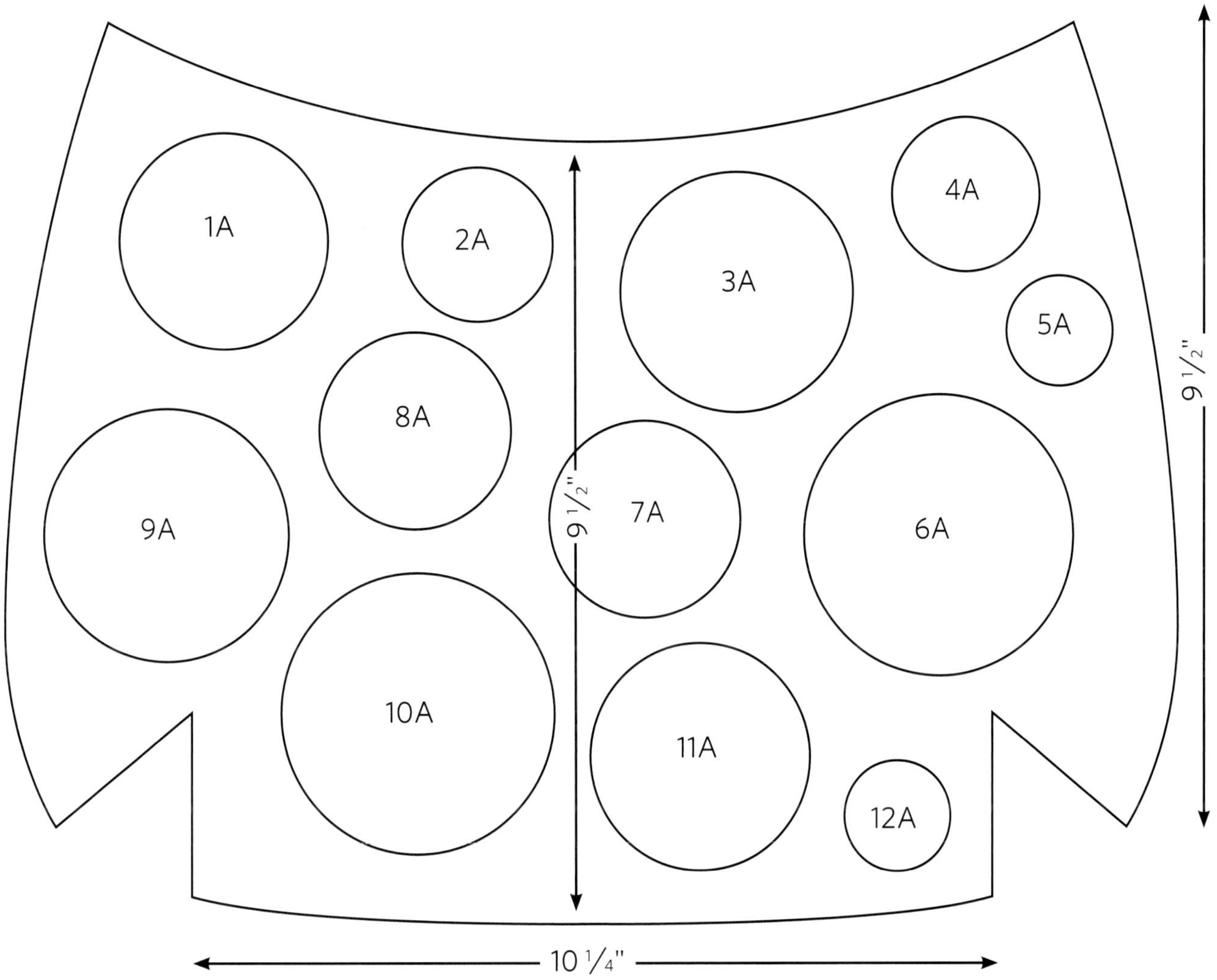

1A
2A
3A
4A
5A
6A
7A
8A
9A
10A
11A
12A
9 ½"
9 ½"
10 ¼"

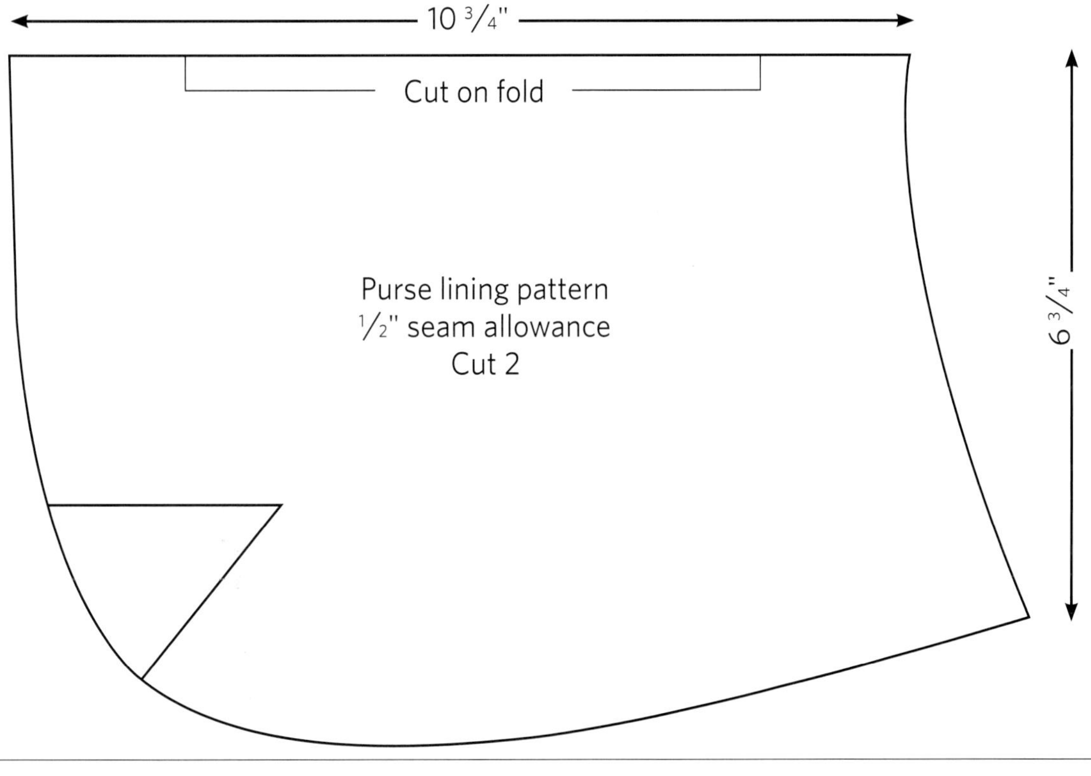

10 ¾"
Cut on fold
Purse lining pattern
½" seam allowance
Cut 2
6 ¾"

Folk Art Flower Travel Tote

Hoot Owl Handbag

"Two for One" Market Bag

18"
15"
12"

East West Clutch

Shading diagram

Milan Bag

Two designs for the Milan Bags shown in this book. Enlarge and expand as you wish for your bag.

The Milan Bag is constructed of 4 sides, each 9" x 8". The bottom of the bag is a square 8" x 8".

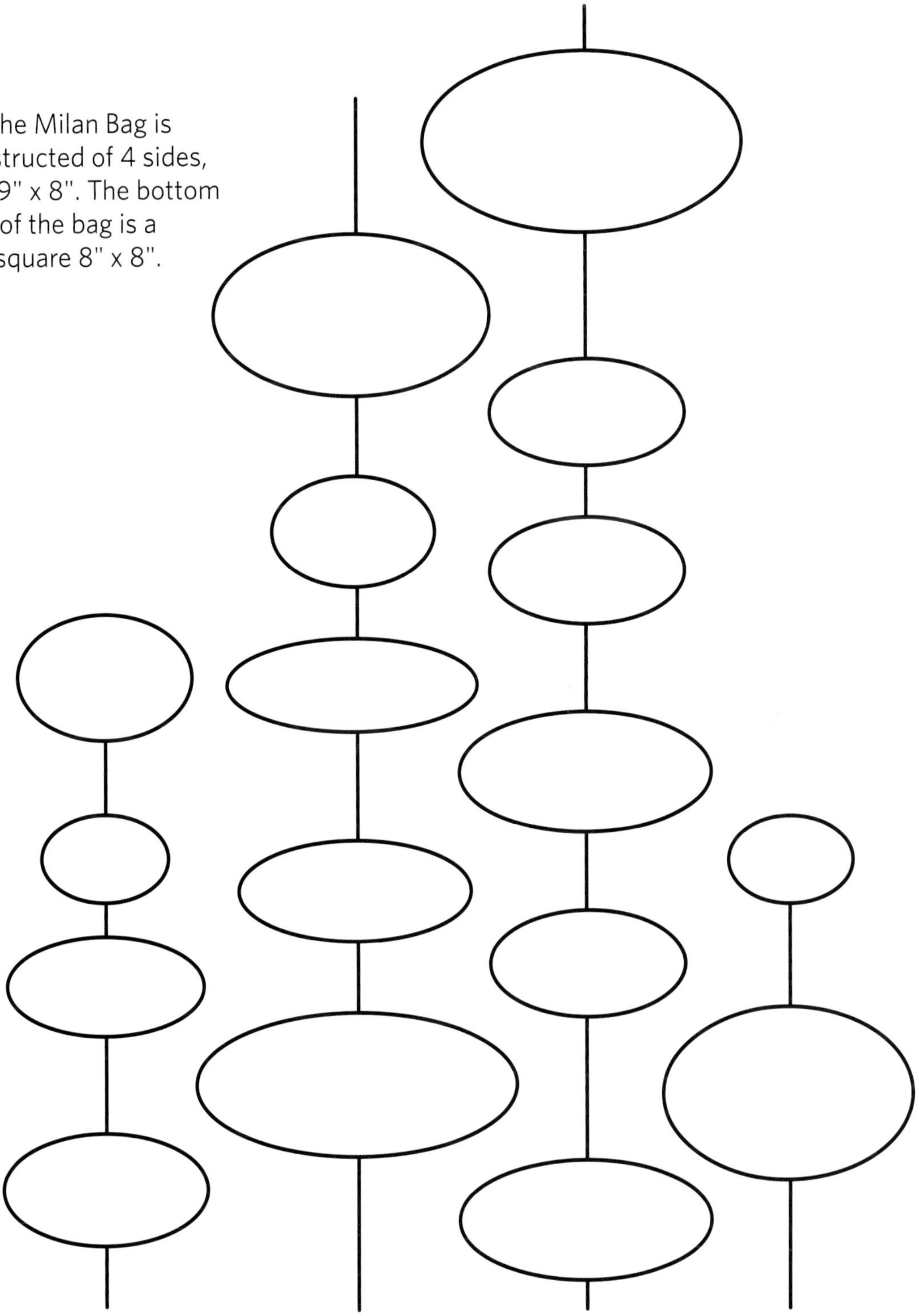

Sunflower Purse

Shading diagram for sunflower

Karma Tree Carpetbag

Note: Dimensions given are for the 8 ½ " internal frame.

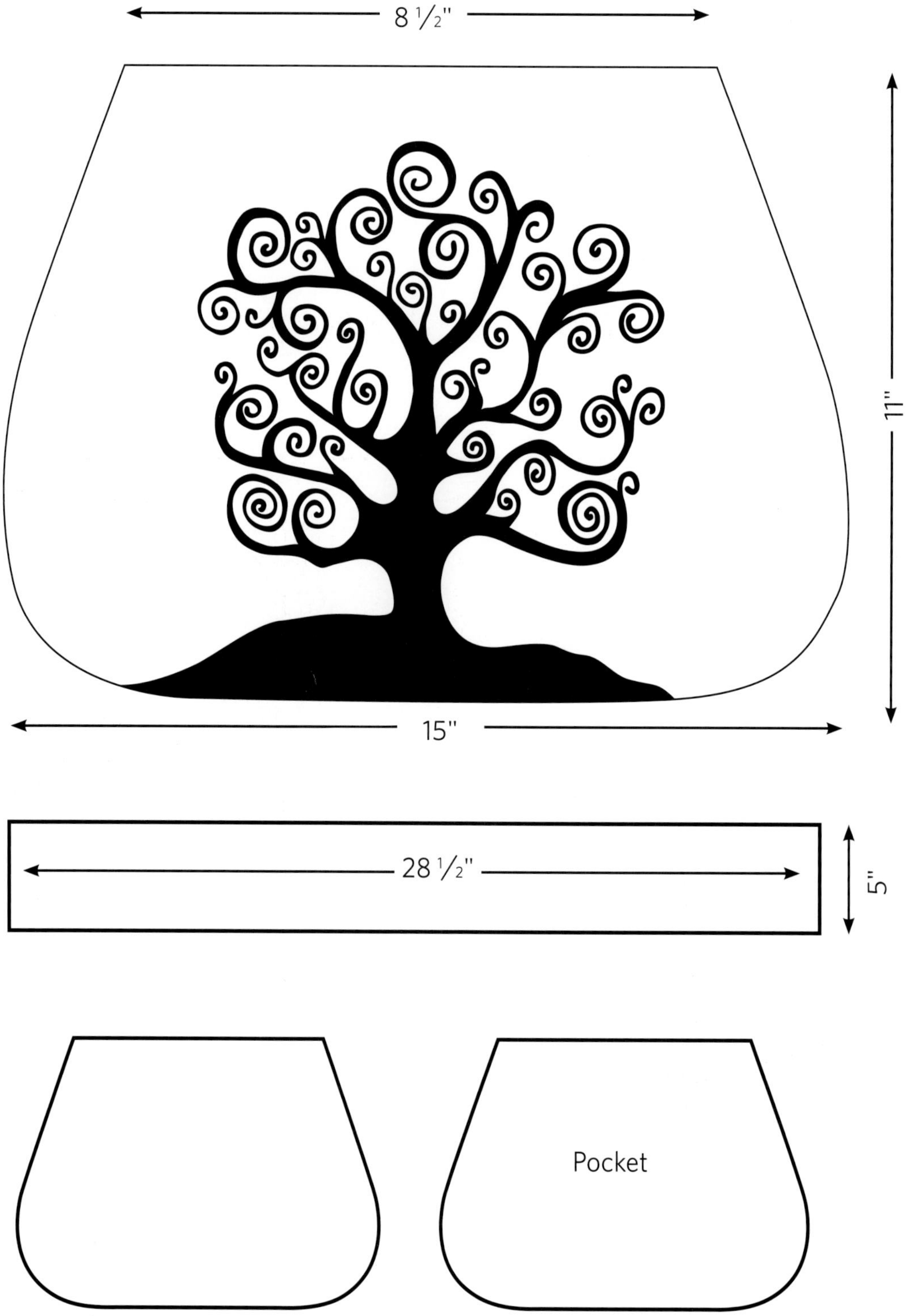

Bliss Bag

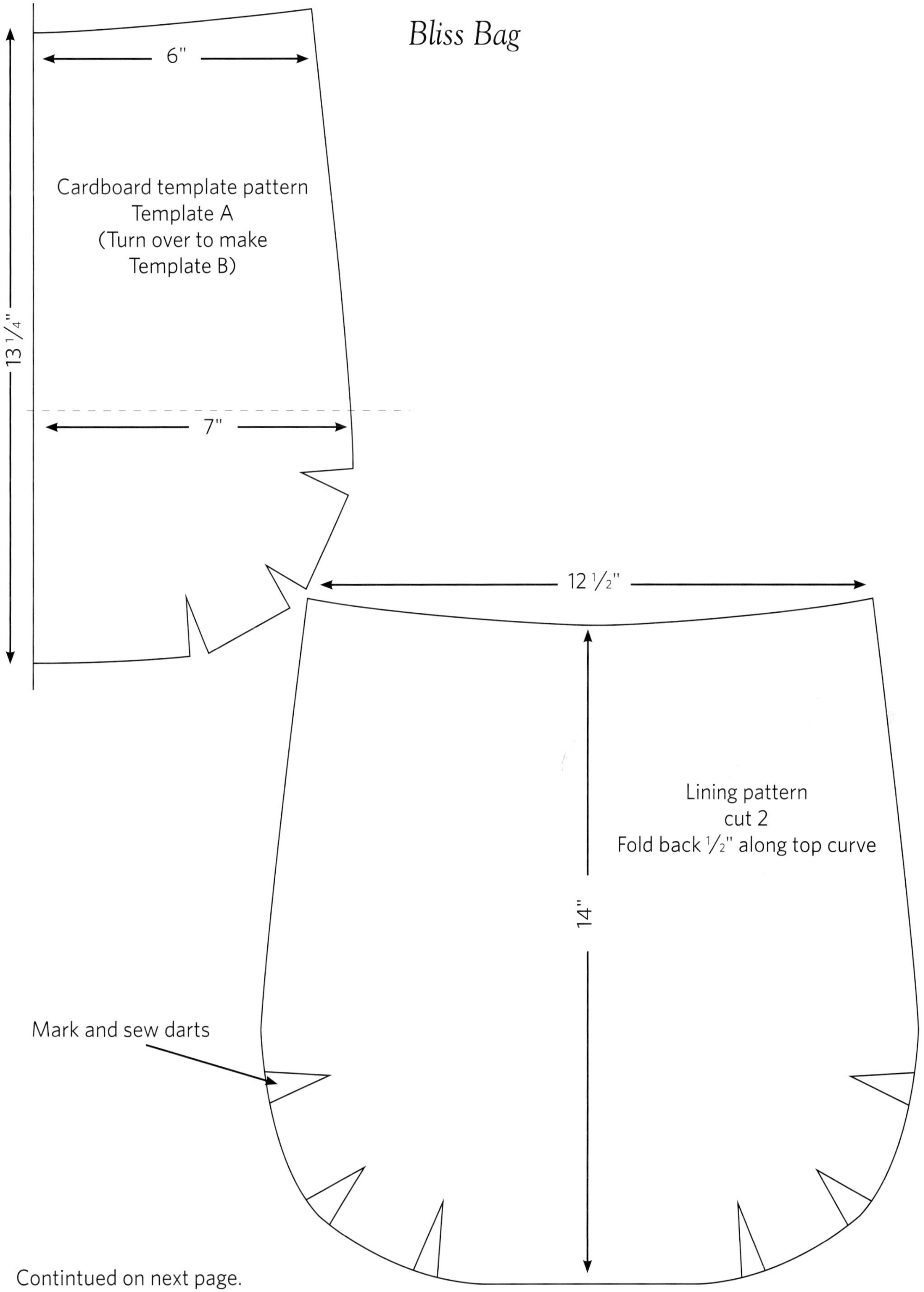

Contintued on next page.

Bliss Bag

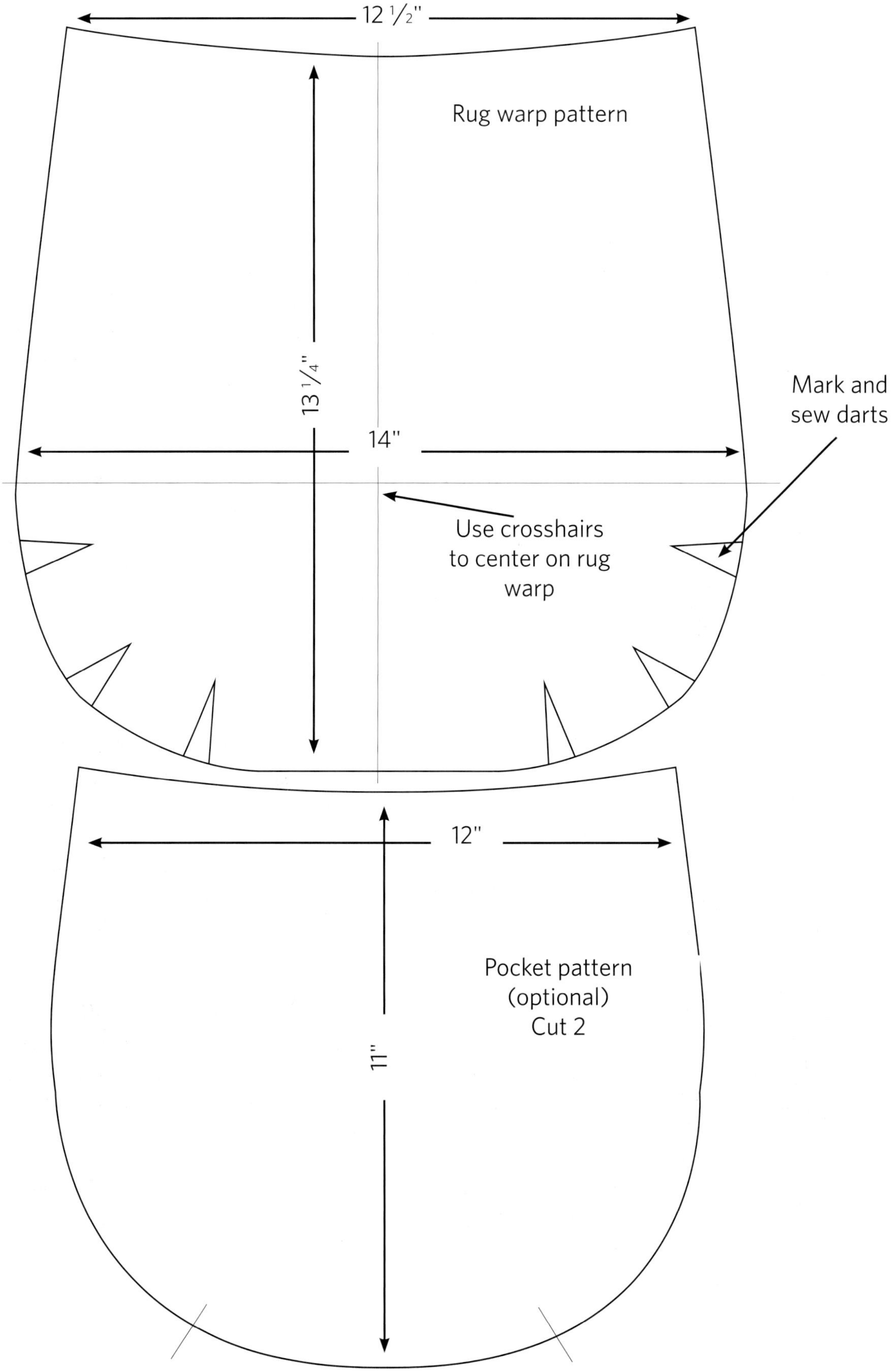

12 1/2"
Rug warp pattern
13 1/4"
14"
Mark and sew darts
Use crosshairs to center on rug warp
12"
Pocket pattern (optional) Cut 2
11"

CONTRIBUTORS

Jen Manuell is an award-winning fourth generation rug hooker, first taught by her aunt, the late Jean Armstrong. Jen started hooking in 1999 and has taught for more than a decade. Jen has traveled all over Canada, the United States, and England, sharing her fresh and distinctive ideas under her own Fish Eye Rugs banner. Her work has been included in many exhibits, in both Canada and the US and has been featured in several publications over the years.

Susan Clarke started hooking 10 years ago, and enjoys attending workshops exploring different hooking styles. She designs many of her own rugs, and lately she is exploring more functional rug media—carpetbags and footstools. She is a member of the Ontario Hooking Craft Guild, and president of the Georgetown Rug Hooking Group.

Jennifer O'Malley holds an art degree and has been hooking rugs for the last 17 years. Originally self-taught, then later seeking out classes, camps, and inspiration from fellow rug hookers, she has designed more than 25 original rugs. Her "Definitely Denim" Pocketbook married her love of sewing, upcycling denim, and rug hooking into a piece of portable art. Jennifer (formerly from Telford, Pennsylvania) now resides in Schwenksville, Pennsylvania, with her husband of 39 years and three cats.

Linda Pietz has been designing needle work for over 40 years. She began with her own line of needlepoint, then designed for companies such as Bucilla and Dimensions. More recently, she has been designing rug hooking patterns for sister Nola Heidbreder's company. Linda has had her work featured in Rug Hooking *magazine,* Woman's Day*, and* Family Circle*. Linda and Nola have two new books due out in 2017. Linda lives in Northern California with her husband, Mark, and Montague the cat. In addition to designing, she teaches a variety of art and fiber art classes.*

Nola Heidbreder teaches rug hooking and fiber art at her studio in St. Louis and across the country. Her specialties are creativity, embellishing, dyeing, recycling in crafting and historic rugs. Her work has been featured in Rug Hooking *magazine and other publications such as* Mary Engelbreit's Home Companion Magazine, ATHA newsletter, Hooked on Rugs, Creative Hooker, Hooked on Wool, Hooked Rugs Today, Finishing Rugs, Contemporary Hooked Rugs, *and in* The "Art" of Playing Cards. *Nola hooked all 44 of the presidents in the 2013 Special Exhibit of Hooked and Knitted Presidents at Sauder Village. The collection received the 2013 Sauder "Collection" Award.*

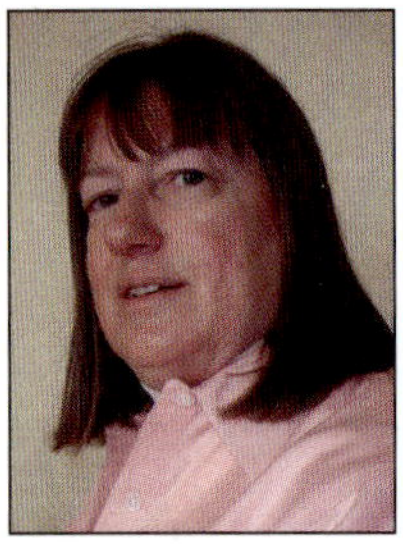

Norma Batastini is the owner of Heart in Hand Rug Hooking and has been passionate about hooking since 1995. She enjoys a variety of styles, cuts, and materials, but wide cut primitives are her favorite. Norma lives in northern New Jersey, a congested melting pot of people and ideas; she brings this energy and vision to her students in classes and workshops around the country. Norma is a frequent contributor to Rug Hooking *magazine and has written about tote bags, molas, and folklife rugs. She is co-director of the popular Rugs by the Sea in Cape May, New Jersey.*

Sharon A. Smith is a graphic designer who has been hooking rugs since 2009. Her rug patterns have been featured in numerous magazine articles. She has published a book, Punchneedle on a Grand Scale *(Martingale Press). She teachers at guilds, biennials, and in her own studio in Walnut Creek, California.*

Ali Strebel has been teaching fiber art nationally and internationally since 1986. Her business, Ali Strebel Designs for Kindred Spirits, is located in Dayton, Ohio, where she sells the line of books and patterns she has published, as well as hand-dyed wool, yarn, roving, and other fiber-art supplies. She specializes in incorporating different techniques and fibers into her rug hooking and teaches others, inspiring them to do the same.

Cindy Irwin has been hooking rugs since 1983. She is a certified McGown teacher and a juried member of the Pennsylvania Guild of Craftsmen; she holds classes in her home and is a traveling teacher. She is president of the Conestoga Guild of McGown Rug Crafters and the assistant director of Northern Teacher's Workshop. (She is currently working on learning how to say, "No.")